AF566994

The Bamboo Basket Art of Higashi Takesonosai

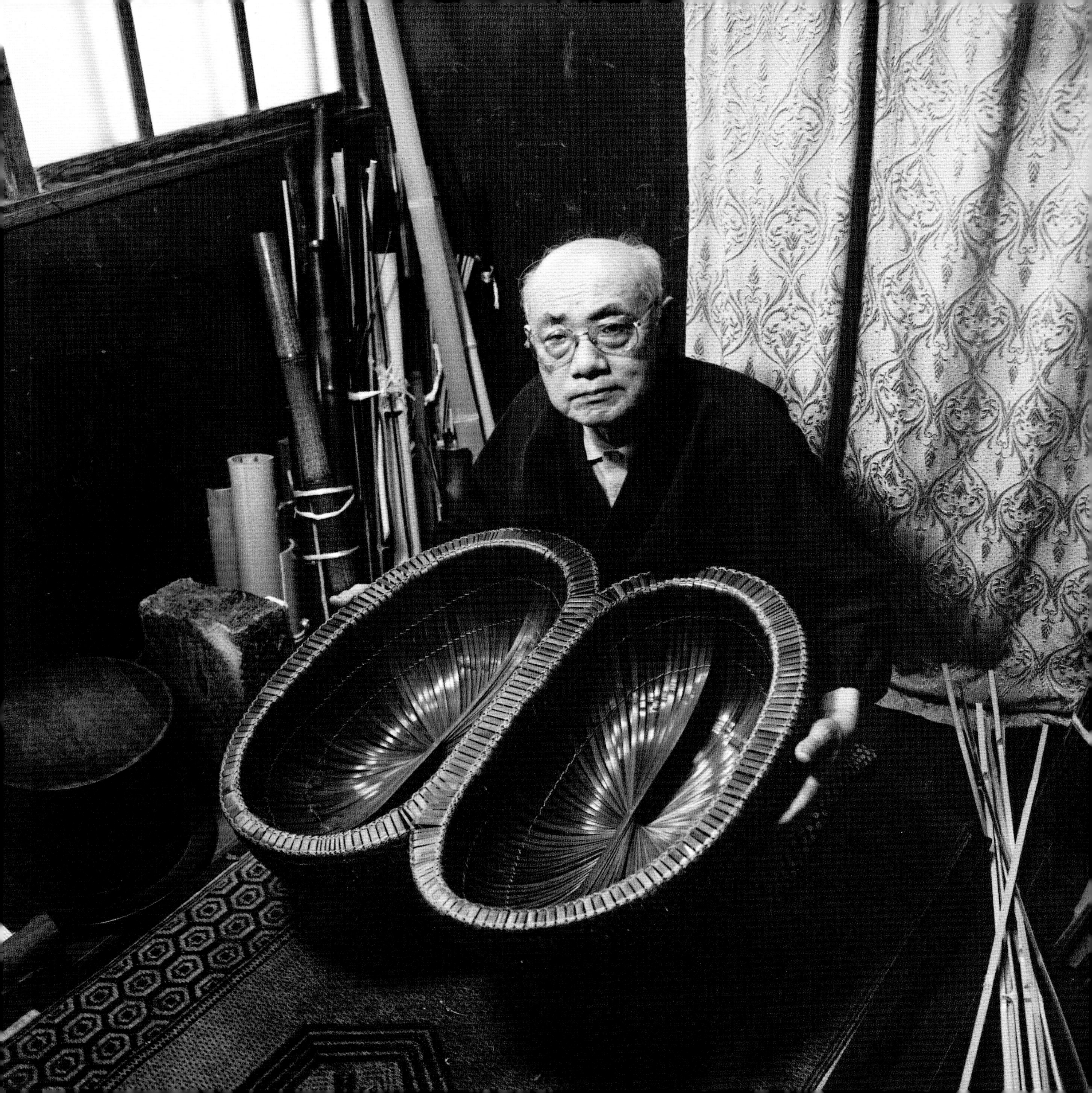

The Bamboo Basket Art of Higashi Takesonosai

Lloyd Cotsen Robert T. Coffland

Photographs by Pat Pollard
Portrait by Art Streiber

COTSEN OCCASIONAL PRESS
Los Angeles 2002

Foreword and Acknowledgements

This is the first book to be published in the West tracing the career of a bamboo artist. It would not have been possible without the extensive collection of Higashi Takesonosai's work that Mr. Cotsen has acquired for over twenty-five years. Higashi kept for himself a small number of pivotal pieces that complete the picture of his post-World War II career but unfortunately, there are no pieces available from prior to the war.

Writing this book has been a tremendous learning experience filled with many challenges. I have become acutely aware of the shortcomings in my efforts to place a single bamboo artist in the sweep of Japanese bamboo art history. The lack of publications on bamboo art in Japanese or English is one of the challenges. Additionally, having seen only a scattering of the Teiten, Nitten, Gendai Kogei, and Shin Kogei exhibition catalogues, my ability to fully place Higashi's work within that context has been somewhat limited. It is my sincere hope that my efforts will stimulate people to do more research and writing on this very important area of Japanese art and culture. It is a very fertile area for scholars on both sides of the Pacific.

The oral and written interviews with Higashi Takesonosai took place over a twelve-month period. Asking direct questions in Japan is not the most polite behavior. Additionally, the time needed for him to recall facts and events is quite long. Some of the dates for when he made various baskets are approximate. I am deeply appreciative of Mr. & Mrs. Higashi in graciously assisting me in what at time must have seemed a very strange task. They were also helpful in pursuing the splendid photographs that were stored in many different places in their home.

This book was only made possible by the help of many people. Yoneyama Yoshiko and Okada Koichiro spent hours interpreting and translating all of my questions. They also provided invaluable assistance in translating the many cultural aspects of what Higashi said. Lyssa Stapleton was endlessly helpful with the logistics of getting the pieces safely back and forth for photography, and in providing information on the baskets. Pat Pollard's deep understanding of how to bring out the beauty of bamboo art makes me want to do another book. I would like to give a special thanks to Art Streiber for allowing the usage of his portrait of Higashi. Rochelle Reed has done an excellent job of editing the text, which has greatly eased the pain of writing for me. Most important is my wife, Mary Hunt Kahlenberg, whose belief in me is priceless.

Lastly, I want to thank Lloyd Cotsen, my co-author, for making this important project happen, and in taking the time to write such a beautiful heartfelt essay. His deep love and appreciation of Japanese bamboo art is palpable. A week never goes by without my thinking how lucky I was that Mr. Cotsen asked me to look for bamboo baskets for him during my trips to Japan.

Robert T. Coffland

Table of Contents

Because of my continued relationship with his family, I dedicate this small volume in memory of their late son, Professor Mashiko Higashi, 1954 to 2000.

Lloyd Cotsen

Personal View of Higashi, The Man and the Artist

By Lloyd Cotsen

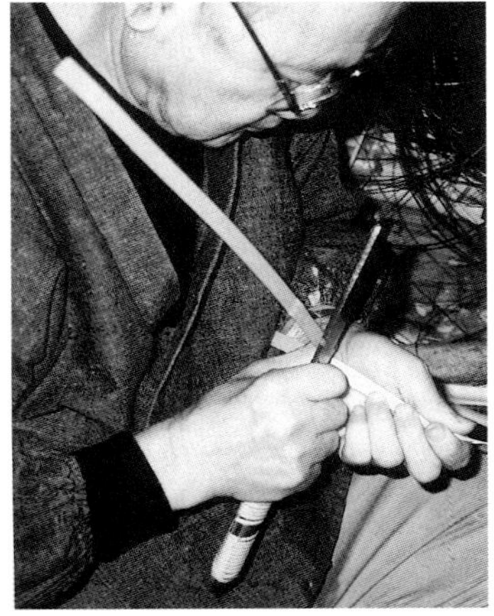

Higashi Takesonosai
Photo by Lloyd Cotsen

It was more than 25 years ago that I first met Mr. Higashi. And I remember it as if it were yesterday.

Through an interpreter, we called from our hotel in Kyoto to introduce ourselves and ask permission to visit. I described myself as a basket collector who wanted to find the teacher of a young craftsman whose basket I had bought in Kyoto. And I was told that he was that teacher.

Graciously Mr. Higashi invited us to his small home and work studio in Kyoto.

He lived on a street limited to pedestrian traffic and bounded by two-story homes built hugging each other. We locate the door number, rang the bell and were greeted by Mr. Higashi. He invited us in and led us upstairs to his studio, which by American standards was almost closet-size.

It was hard to believe that he could achieve such artistic results in this confining space. Basket boxes were piled on all sides. Bundles of cut bamboo were stored at the rear of a water closet and heater. The room was probably only a four or six tatami mat-sized space.

Mr. Higashi's wife followed us upstairs with tea and cakes. As we sat, we talked about baskets, my interest in baskets and in particular, his baskets. He would then bring out a few, one by one.

What particularly attracted me, and still does, to Mr. Higashi's baskets is his spatial sense as expressed by his mastery of the material. As I looked at each basket, I had a feeling of being part of a controlled adventure in space.

Then, as now, his ability to express volume, and at the same time stretch the technical limits of bamboo, made his work exciting to me. Through his technical virtuosity with bamboo, aided by his respect for traditional concepts, his work achieved an expressive spatial impact. Both with my eye and my hands, I felt I had discovered an artist who simultaneously could create within the Japanese tradition and yet appeal to Western sensibilities, or at least to mine.

Since my first contact with Mr. Higashi and over the following many years and many visits, I have collected more than 30 of his works. Now I am running out of space. Fortunately for my crowded storage and exhibition room, Mr. Higashi is slowing down in terms of his own output. But he still continues to make a few gems a year…all of which continue to tempt me.

Within each of his baskets, I see a romantic representation of the spirit of his artistry which captures elements of nature like moving water, immutable rocks, and bending bamboo, all so important to the Japanese aesthetic tradition and thus represented in my collection.

I guess that is why, on first seeing them, I responded so favorably to his baskets, which became the initial focus of my collection of contemporary bamboo baskets (or more accurately, bamboo sculptures). When I see Mr. Higashi cutting his bamboo strips, shaping them, tying them, and weaving these slips into a meaningful shape, I marvel both at his ability to conceptualize and at the strength of his hands in achieving that form. Even more, I marvel at his vision… his sense of what I think of as bamboo engineering to achieve such forms, all from just one natural material. Wow!

Over the years, our relationship became more personal. We began to call on Mr. Higashi and visit with him and his family whenever we were in Kyoto. After viewing his baskets, we would walk down to a small restaurant and celebrate my purchases (or his sales!). I knew I felt good; and I think he felt recognized for the artist he is.

As our relationship deepened, he would bring his young son, Mashiko, to join us and interpret. I saw Mashiko grow up, finish the university, marry, have children and then become a professor of ecology at Kyoto University. Once when Mashiko visited Los Angeles with his family, I had the opportunity to meet and have lunch with them. It is a poignant memory for me because it was the last time I saw him before he died unexpectedly on a research project in Mexico. What a tragedy for Mr. and Mrs. Higashi and Mashiko's family.

I feel that some of the light and energy that Mr. Higashi had shown in his earlier baskets were dimmed by Mashiko's death. Yet he kept making baskets and exhibiting them. Last year, I felt that his spirits had revived, perhaps aided by the recognition that is at last coming to him. And that is what I hope this book will do for him as well.

Mr. Higashi is very modest. I want him to know that he is primarily responsible for my ever-expanding interest in Japanese bamboo baskets and for my particular interest in baskets by contemporary bamboo artists. While buying baskets from Mr. Higashi, I learned a great deal. I became aware of not just the basket, but also the spirit of the artist and the complexity of the art.

He heightened my awareness of the subtle differences of shape and texture in bamboo. I learned to recognize that baskets were not just objects, but objects that could communicate feelings and sensitivities expressed by the artist. A quiet man in public, Mr. Higashi let his baskets and work speak for him. And they spoke to me.

I am most indebted to him for starting me on my way on a journey through the changing and developing world of contemporary Japanese bamboo baskets.

Looking back over these years, I cannot think of Kyoto without thinking of Mr. Higashi working away in his small studio, creating shapes out of his own imagination and his own intuitive understanding of what can be achieved with just one material, natural bamboo. What he has achieved is awe-inspiring, in terms of not just the number of baskets he has made but also the variety, the craftsmanship, and the creativity of those baskets. His feet may be on the ground, but his head is in the heavens which is where, I suspect, he gets his inspiration.

Thank you, Higashi-san, for enriching my life with your vision of beauty. I will make sure that your baskets will be seen by future generations because they are to be given to a museum, the Asian Art Museum of San Francisco, and will be part of their permanent collection.

A Life with Bamboo

By Robert T. Coffland

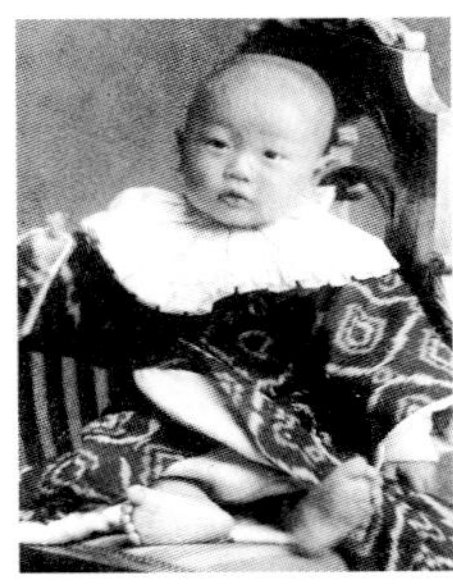

1915, Higashi's baby picture

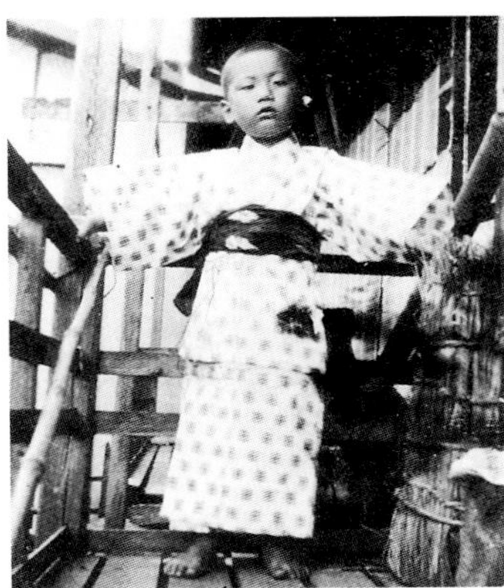

1920, Higashi's birthday picture taken on his uncle's farm

Higashi Takesonosai's earliest memories of bamboo involve summers spent on his uncle's farm. He was six. There he would see people making simple rough baskets for daily use. More importantly, he and his cousins would make kites and other toys out of green bamboo they collected around the farm. As Higashi remembers, a beautiful sound came from wind blowing through the grove.

Higashi was born on July 28, 1915, in the eastern area of Kyoto. His parents, Seijiro and Tsui, were originally from Shiga prefecture, which is west of Lake Biwa. Seijiro was the third son in a prosperous farming family and as his inheritance, his father built a liquor store in Kyoto for Seijiro to manage. There were living quarters upstairs. Higashi was the firstborn; a brother and sister would soon follow.

Higashi started his schooling in Kyoto but when he was eight, his mother became seriously ill, and she was hospitalized. Higashi was sent to live with his uncle's family in Shiga Prefecture. He lived there for three happy years. He and his cousins would spend hours playing in the countryside. The boys occasionally made bamboo traps to catch game birds to eat. One day they made kites out of green bamboo cut from a special bamboo forest kept for sale to wholesalers. When his uncle found out, he was furious. But his uncle's anger turned to amusement when Higashi explained that he wanted to use that green bamboo because it made a better kite.

In school, Higashi was exposed to painting, drawing and calligraphy. When he was 11, one of his teachers advised him that he should consider becoming an artist. At about this time, his mother's health improved, and he moved back to Kyoto. This same year, his father took him to the Kyoto Museum to see his first art exhibition. This was the start of regular visits to museums and galleries, a practice that has continued throughout his life. At the Kyoto Museum, he saw a painting by Yamamoto Shunkyo of three chicks under an umbrella. He was deeply taken with their life-like quality, which further fueled his desire to be an artist.

Shortly after Higashi returned to Kyoto, his father's health failed, eventually forcing the sale of the liquor store. Now Higashi would have to help support his family but at the same time, his artistic skills were growing and he dreamed of becoming an artist. In his last year of school, he took an examination to study with Yamamoto Shunkyo, the artist whose work he had admired at the Kyoto Museum. Higashi was accepted as an apprentice, but this meant ten years of studying with Yamamoto without pay. His father objected — the family needed money. And even after ten years of apprenticeship, his father pointed out, it was questionable how much money Higashi could earn as a painter.

A bamboo artisan by the name of Kaneko Chikukosai lived in Higashi's neighborhood. He made baskets on order from tea ceremony dealers; he never created anything for submission to art exhibitions. His baskets were woven in the wagumi style, simple and rough in appearance. This type of basket drew deeply on Japanese traditions dating back to the Jomon period, about 5,000 BC. At the urging of Kaneko's wife, Higashi began visiting the bamboo artisan. Higashi was fascinated with the process of making a basket, and especially how the rim was finished. When Higashi graduated from school at 15, Kaneko asked him if he would consider learning basket making. He had never had an apprentice, and he did not have a son. Higashi agreed to try. Higashi's father was very pleased at this news because from the start, there would be a salary. Even though basket making was much lower in status than painting, his father said, at least he could make a living.

At first, Higashi was ambivalent about working with bamboo because of his desire to be a painter. But Kaneko was a patient teacher, and Higashi was an exceptional student. Kaneko began his lessons by having Higashi weave the body of baskets, instructing him to make things a little looser or tighter. Next, Kaneko taught him how to prepare the bamboo, and then how to make the base and finish the rim. For the next three years, Higashi settled into a routine of going to his master's house at 8 a.m. and working until 6 p.m. At this time, people typically had the first and fifteenth days of month off. On those free days, Higashi continued painting and drawing, and he visited art museums and exhibitions. Becoming a painter was still in his mind.

Higashi was such a good student that Kaneko would leave him alone in the afternoons and go off to the theater. Higashi enjoyed working with his master, as Kaneko had a happy and sunny disposition. From him, Higashi learned that the earth is always turning so he must keep growing and developing as a human being. Eventually he realized that he wanted to learn more about the technique of basketry. When he met the wife of Wada Rinshinsai, a famous Kyoto bamboo artisan, she suggested that he study with her husband. Kaneko was supportive of this move — he knew that Higashi had great potential.

At about this time, Higashi began to feel a strong spiritual bond with bamboo and basket making: He stopped eating bamboo shoots, a great Japanese springtime delicacy, believing that if bamboo was going to be the source of his livelihood, he should respect its life. He continued this self-imposed ban until he turned 75. Only when his health began to decline, did he once again eat the delectable shoots so that he could "become one with bamboo."

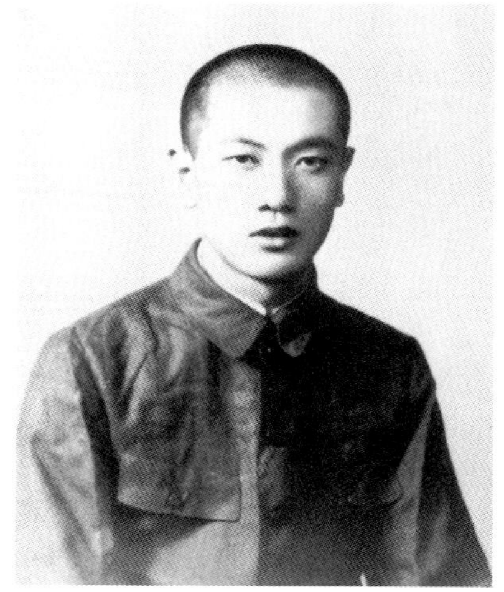

1935, Higashi as a young man

When Higashi began working with Wada, his family moved into the Wadas' neighborhood, buying the house where Higashi still lives. Like Kaneko, Wada was an artisan who made baskets by order for tea ceremony dealers and like Kaneko, he never created works for exhibitions. His flower baskets were in the karamono style, which draws on Chinese tradition, and his work was technically dazzling. As a teacher, however, he was strict and critical, very different than Kaneko. Once when Higashi had finished a basket, Wada squeezed the rim and heard a sound, then made Higashi redo the entire rim. But from his stern master, Higashi learned the importance self discipline and he learned to have a deep belief in what he was creating.

Higashi's work routine was much the same with Wada as it had been with Kaneko. On his own time, he continued to paint and go to museums and exhibitions. During this period, he visited an exhibition where he saw the work of Maeda Chikubosai I and Tanabe Chikuunsai I, who were two of the best know artists in the Kansai region. Their work did not move him, but he admired the technical artistry of their baskets. He began to think that he could make baskets with more style and originality. He realized he did not like simply making copies of traditional baskets. During his free time, Higashi began to create baskets of his own design. Often he would work all night to complete a piece for exhibition. In 1937, he received his first acceptance to exhibit at the Kyoto Art and Craft Exhibition. This led to commissions for two baskets for the son of the head priest at Kyoto's Honganji temple. During this time he found a circle of artistic friends, and he began to think he might become a bamboo artist until he could become a painter.

Highashi hid his ambitions from Wada, because he knew that his teacher would not approve. Wada had told him that if he submitted his work to Bunten, the forerunner of the Nitten exhibition, he would fire him. Wada felt no one should judge another's work, even for exhibition. This led to Higashi starting to think he wanted to become independent. A new dream began to form in his mind and that was to make bamboo baskets that would be seen as art. At the same time, he knew that he would have to find a way to support his family. His financial responsibility had a positive side — as the sole support for his parents and siblings, he was excused from military service. In 1937, after three years with Wada, he left to start his own business.

In the same year, Higashi assumed the artistic name of Takesonosai, which literally means, "Made by bamboo garden." This came about because of a relationship between Higashi's father and Prince Konoe, a member of the extended Imperial family. At the time of his son's declaration of independence, Higashi's father sought the Prince's advice for a name. Prince Konoe felt if Higashi was to be the king of the bamboo world, he should have a royal name, explaining that in ancient China, the Emperor was called "Take no Sonou" which means "born in the bamboo garden." The Japanese Imperial Family had appropriated the phrase for the Japanese Emperor, but as Prince Konoe was a member of the Imperial family, there was no chance of offense if Higashi assumed the name. Years later, Iizuka Rokansai, the most original bamboo artist of the first half of the twentieth century, told Higashi that he wanted to use the same name but was fearful of offending the Emperor and the Imperial Family.

Since Higashi could not go to either Kaneko's or Wada's clients for basket orders, he visited other tea ceremony shops in the Osaka and Kyoto area. Because of the range of basket styles he had learned, he was able to start building clients for his work. Within three years, he had established business relationships with two prominent tea ceremony stores that would last until the middle of the 1980's. In order to fully understand the needs of his customers, Higashi privately studied the matcha and sencha tea ceremonies. Also, he made a scrapbook of the different types of bamboo baskets that his customers might possibly choose. His flexibility in meeting the needs of his customers gave him a necessary economic foundation, and he began to think about creating his own original artwork.

In 1940, Higashi first saw the work of Iizuka Rokansai, and was convinced that bamboo basket making could be art, not craft. This added to his conviction that he could be an artist who worked with bamboo as his medium. And yet in the back of his mind, he still wanted to be a painter. In 1941, he submitted his first piece to the Bunten exhibition, and it was accepted. Because of the war and his financial situation, however, he was unable to go to Tokyo. Higashi knew that it was inevitable he would be drafted. Since his family was dependent on him, he was busily building a stock of baskets for them to sell during his absence.

Higashi was drafted in 1944 and sent to China. Shortly after his arrival, he became sick and was hospitalized for almost a year. Upon his recovery, he served as a clerk in the regional headquarters. Higashi was very concerned about his family's well being and started to miss bamboo basket making. During his stay, he observed local utilitarian basket making that used bamboo and willow. On one occasion, he visited a wealthy local Chinese family who showed him lacquered bamboo baskets. These experiences gave him ideas about what he might create in the future.

In 1945, Higashi's father died. Not being able to be with his mother and siblings to grieve was very hard. The war ended in 1945, but it wasn't until January 1947 that Higashi returned. Japan was devastated, but Higashi was happy to be back with his family and at work in his studio. Orders from his clients began to slowly come back. Like many Japanese at this time, Higashi worked seven days a week to make enough money to survive. Additionally, severe food shortages throughout Japan meant that he was continually going out to visit his uncle's farm in Shiga Prefecture for rice and other staples. During one of his visits in 1948, he was introduced to Morie Toshie and within the year, she would become his wife. Mrs. Higashi comes from a thirteen-generation landowning family. They have often joked about her coming from a large, traditional family farm to a tiny house in Eastern Kyoto. In the 1949, Higashi's mother died. Sadly, Higashi acknowledged their deaths had a positive side — now he was responsible only for his new

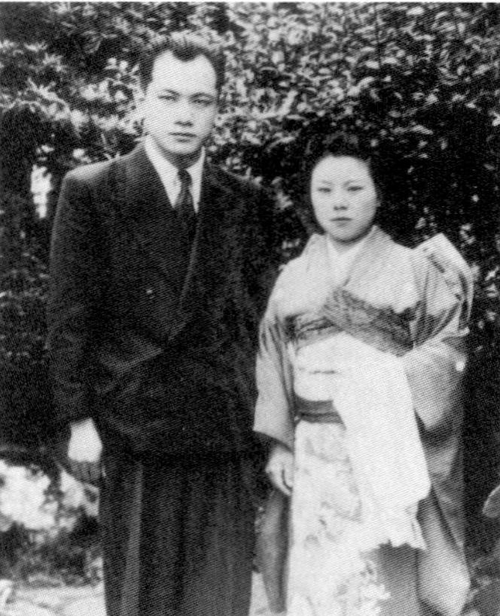

1949, wedding picture of Higashi and his wife Toshie

wife and himself. This would allow him to save money so that he could take the necessary two to three months of time to create masterworks for exhibitions.

In the early 1950's, Higashi's orders steadily grew. His first son, Kiyokazu, was born at this time. Now he began to think about submitting work for exhibition once again. Part of this process was to seek the advice and counsel of leading artists he admired. These artists worked in a variety of mediums including bamboo and were recognized for their excellence by other artists, museums and collectors. Higashi wanted to learn their philosophy and approach to the creation of art. Higashi expanded his artistic horizons beyond painting to studying the work of ceramic and metal artists for inspiration. He understood, he said, that if you use the ideas of other bamboo artists as a starting point, all you get is criticism and the strong possibility of having your submissions rejected.

The first bamboo basket Higashi entered for the Nitten exhibition in 1952 caused a tremendous stir (Figure 1). The piece included the image of butterflies in the body instead of traditional geometric patterns. His desire was to create a basket that included elements of painting. His weaving technique, combined with the fineness of the cut bamboo, meant that he could only complete two centimeters a day. Even after fifty years, Higashi touches this masterwork like a parent touches a child.

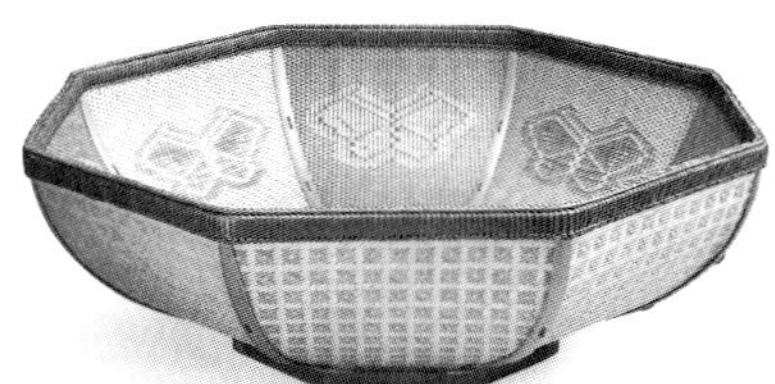

Figure 1

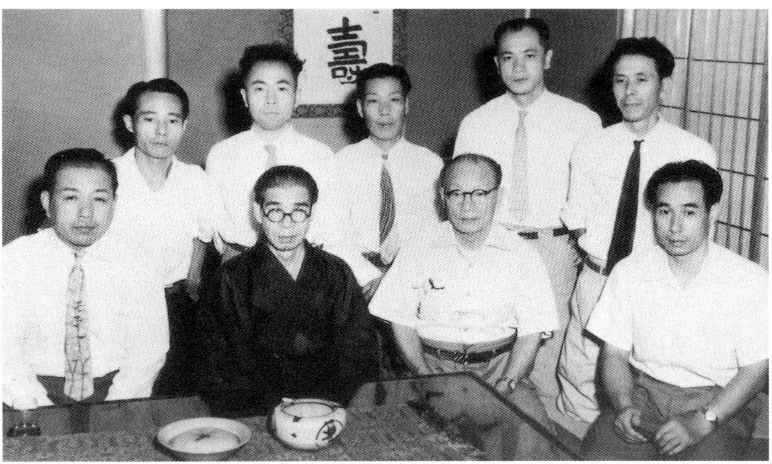

1955, Bamboo artist group at Takashimaya Department Store, Tokyo. Pictured: front row – Tanabe Chikuunsai II, Iizuka Rokansai, Shitazaki Fusai, Iizuka Shokansai; back row – Suemura Shobun, Tanaka Kosai, Maeda Chikubosai II, Higashi Takesonosai, Ito Nobukata

For his 1953 submission to Nitten, he created another finely woven piece with images of crabs and flowers. Higashi nearly won a coveted Toksen Prize for the work. The prize ended up being given to Tanabe Chikuunsai II in honor of his greater experience and senior position in the organization. This was not a total surprise, given Higashi was only 37 years old. More importantly, the bamboo artist, Iizuka Rokansai publicly praised the excellence of his work. This gave Higashi great confidence and inspiration. He now saw himself as an artist with a bright future. At this time, Higashi established two goals for himself. First, he wanted to create artwork that would endure beyond his lifetime. Secondly, he wanted to win a Toksen. In the same year, Rokansai suggested bamboo artists form a group that would meet once a year at the opening of the Nitten exhibition in Tokyo. This group would continue until Rokansai's death in 1957, and was a very important opportunity for Higashi to interact with senior artists.

In 1954, the Higashi's second son, Masahiko, was born. By this time, Higashi was settling into a routine of working typically twelve to fourteen hours a day, a pattern that would continue until the 1980's. Higashi's son, Kiyokazu, told me recently he often wondered as a child how his father could work so hard; Higashi worked six days a week, only taking off Sundays in order to rest and protect his health. At this same time, he set the difficult yearly goal of making two pieces for exhibition and about 30 smaller bamboo baskets for tea ceremony dealers. It typically took Higashi three months to make an exhibition piece. During this period, he would not make baskets for his tea ceremony customers, which irritated them. Fortunately, his work was in such demand that his customers tolerated his need to make art. However, because none of his exhibition pieces were sold, it was extremely difficult to balance the family's financial state. Having a strong supportive and loving wife was a great asset.

In the 1950's, Shono Shounsai, who was to later become the first Living National Treasure of Japan in bamboo arts, started to explore new dimensions in sculpture through bamboo. The physical space Shono created in his sculptural work was a breathtaking break with past traditions. Another point of Shono's work was using only the natural color of the bamboo. All of this had a tremendous impact on Japanese bamboo artists, including Higashi. He began to realize the limitations of his karamono style weaving, and wanted to start expressing the life and energy he felt in bamboo. He had always loved how bamboo grows straight, how it bends under the weight of snow. The space between the bamboo in a grove became something he wanted to express in his work.

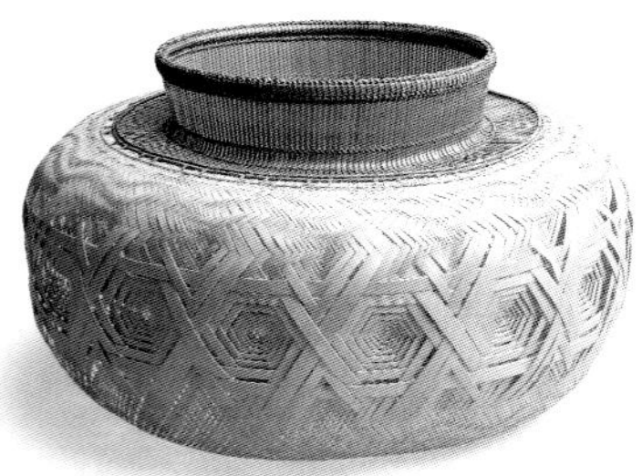

Figure 2

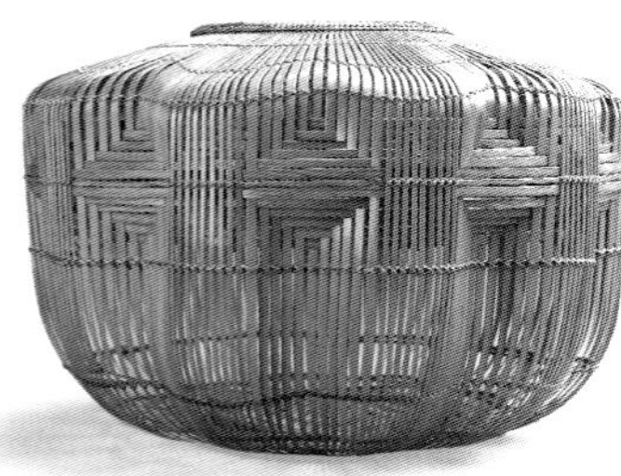

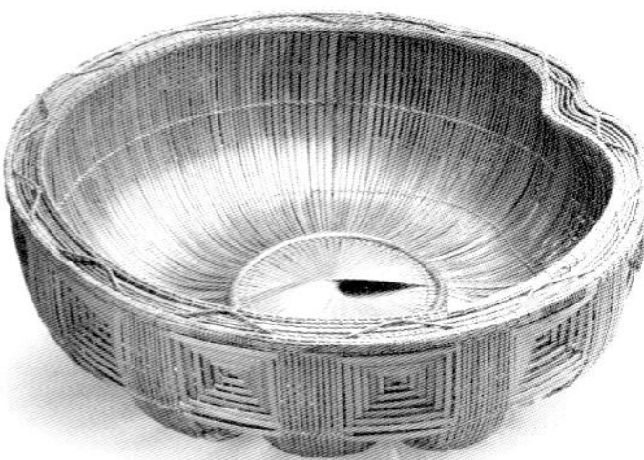

Figure 3

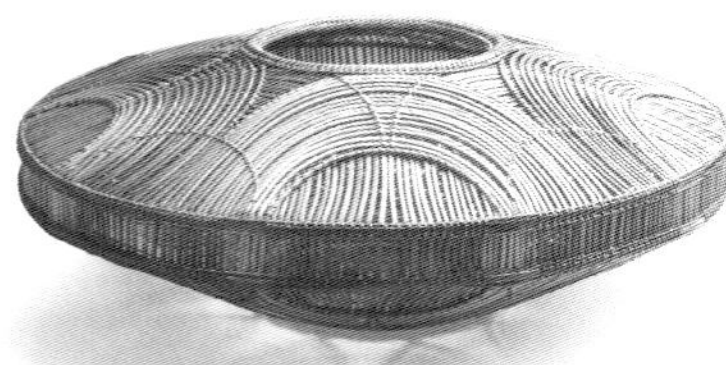

Figure 4

A realization went deep inside him that bamboo had qualities for artistic expression that metal, clay and paint lacked. His commitment to bamboo as his artistic medium was now complete.

Higashi's desire to break away from his earlier weaving style began showing up in 1955. His goal in this basket was to capture the beauty of a hexagonal snow crystal (Figure 2). The use of leached bamboo combined with a minimal amount of dyed bamboo was the influence of Shono. This basket was also the first step towards the development of a unique architectural style of stacking and plaiting the bamboo that eventually became one of his signature techniques (Figure 3).

In 1958, the bamboo artists' group formed by Rokansai dissolved due to political infighting. Artists in Kyoto and Osaka decided to form an organization to build awareness of bamboo art. The group was led by Tanabe Chikuunsai II and met every three months plus they began taking a yearly trip to relax and socialize. More importantly, they started doing a yearly group exhibition at a local department store, and establishing a stronger presence at the local art exhibitions.

At about this time, Kyoto's governor, Ninagawa Torazo, became interested in bamboo and a great supporter of local artists. In late 1950's, Ninagawa was responsible for the government purchase of a major piece by Higashi that was given to Russia's Kiev Museum. Thirty-six years later, Higashi would make a similar piece, now in the Cotsen collection (Figure 4). There would be an additional nine pieces that were purchased by the prefectural government. These purchases encouraged him to continue developing his artwork; the sale of these exhibition pieces gave Higashi greater financial stability. At this time, Higashi still had his two goals for his artistic career. The first and most important was to make artwork that would endure beyond his lifetime. The second was to win the Toksen award at the Nitten exhibition. However, Higashi decided that he would not go about this in the normal way, which involved politics and entertaining senior members. When his work won a Toksen, he decided, it would be solely on its artistic merits. In order to achieve his goals, Higashi knew he would need to create and utilize additional new techniques. This remains a goal for all bamboo artists to this day, but few succeed.

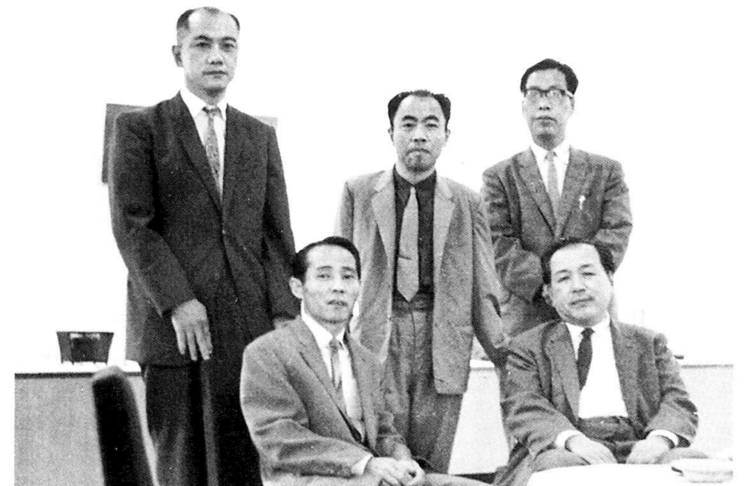

1966, Osaka Kyoto bamboo artists group exhibition at Takashimaya Department Store, Osaka. Pictured: seated – Kimura Shokon and Tanabe Chikuunsai II; standing – Higashi Takesonosai, Tanaka Kosai, Maeda Chikubosai II

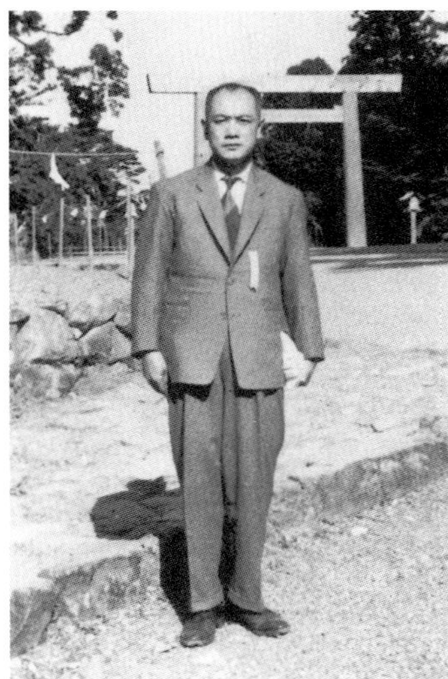

1963, Higashi at Ise Shrine

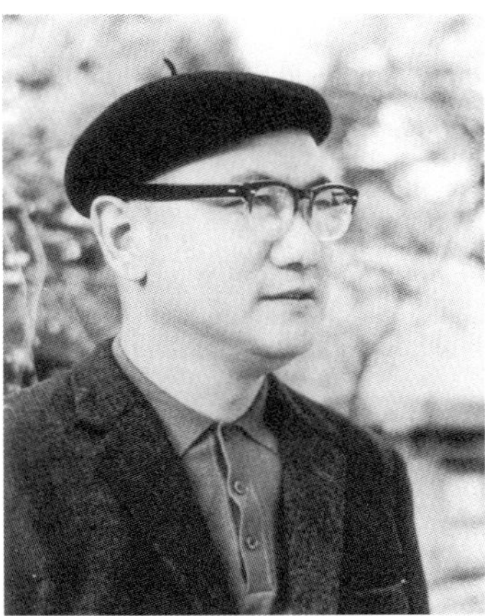

1969, Higashi on trip to Kanazawa

In 1964, Higashi developed a technique that involved stacking strips of bamboo and gradually splaying them to form a spiral (Figure 5). This construct became the interior base of the basket. The strips were brought up, and then this was nested in another basket and a rim made to join the two. This style of basket is dazzling in that the eye of viewer is drawn at once to the interior and architectural surface of the exterior. In same year, Higashi began to exhibit his experimental work in the springtime Gendai Kogei exhibition, less stringently judged than the fall Nitten exhibition. Higashi also began to extensively use smoked bamboo from the rafters of old Japanese farmhouses. Then in 1966, he decided to completely eliminate the traditional basket rim with its knotted rattan finish by bending over the exterior basket body into the inner basket (Figure 6). This gave the impression of the basket flowing endlessly into itself.

These ideas were combined brilliantly in 1971 in Higashi's creation of "Pair" (Figure 7). He decided that he would work on a much larger scale than he normally worked. Further more, he would interlace two vessels made of smoked bamboo. The effect is stunning. There is no beginning or end apparent to the naked eye. Even now Higashi wonders how he made it. Upon completion of "Pair," he knew he would win his Toksen, and he did. Higashi's Toksen gave him a new level of confidence and recognition. There is, in fact, a set formula that artists use in raising their prices upon winning important awards. A second Toksen bestows full Nitten membership. However, Higashi knew that without becoming active in the politics of Nitten, he do not have a chance at winning a second Toksen, which would earn him full membership. He had achieved his goal his way, and that was enough for him.

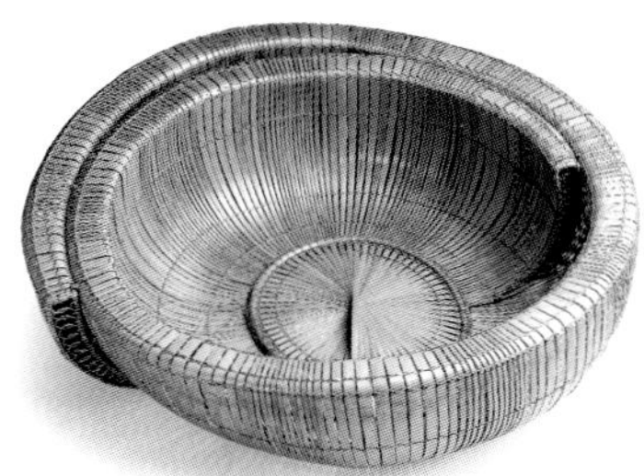

Figure 5

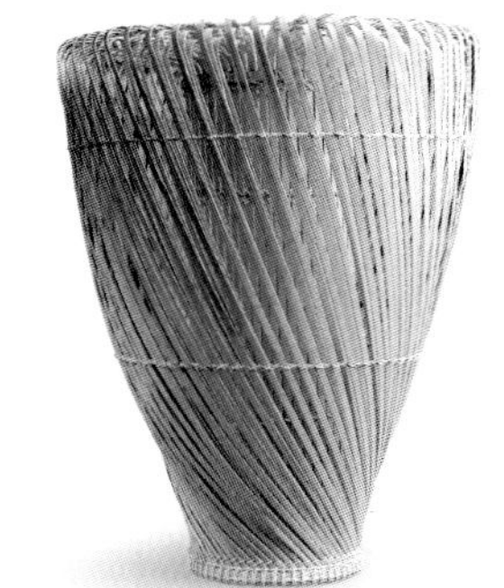

Figure 6

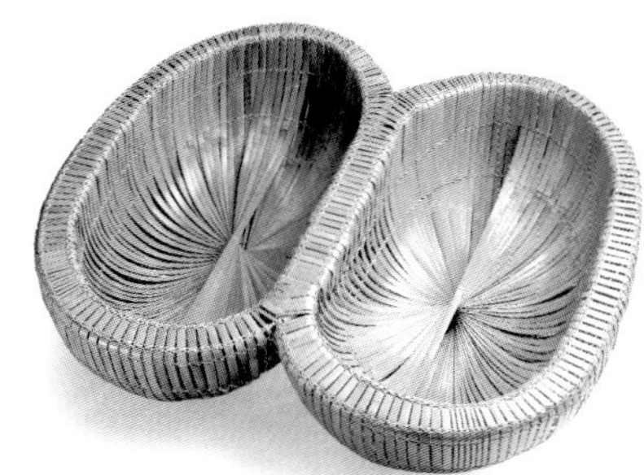

Figure 7

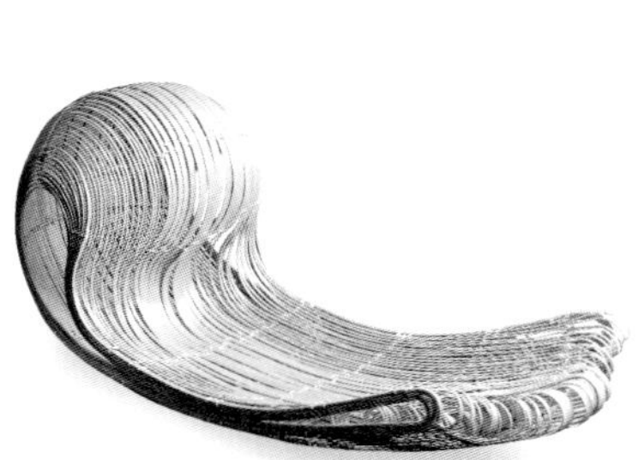

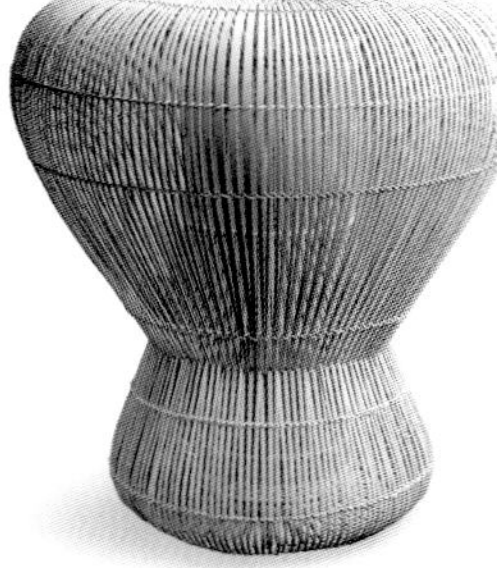

Figure 8

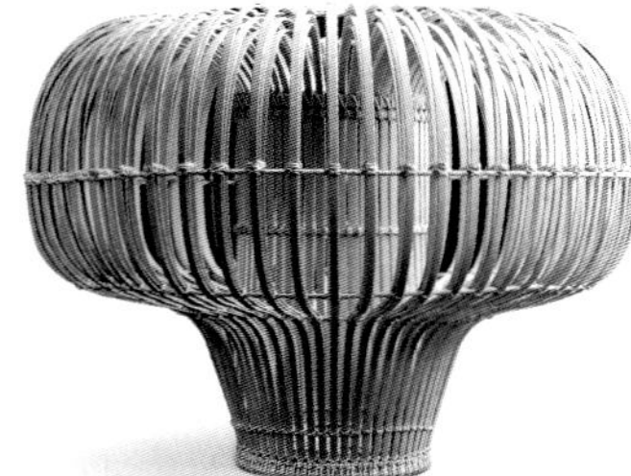

Figure 9

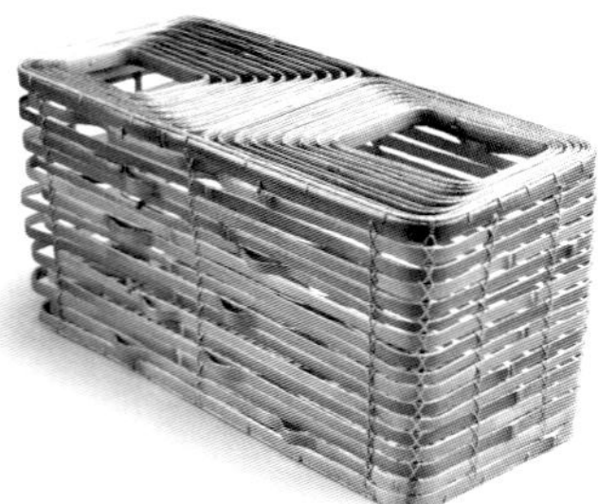

Figure 10

The winning of the Toksen Prize gave Higashi a new sense of artistic freedom that led to a great creative burst in the 1970's. In a sense, he was able to relax and give fuller range to his ideas about the nature of bamboo. This is best illustrated in the lyrical beauty of "Wave" and "Sunlight" (Figure 8). The flowing characteristic of bamboo was powerfully reinterpreted in "Pure Spring (Figure 9). In the mid-1970's, Higashi developed a new artistic technique. Bending bamboo with heat from either an oil lamp or candle, depending on the thickness of the bamboo, he then used this bent bamboo as a geometric accent in baskets such as "Cliff" (Figure 10). In 1976, Higashi had his first solo show at Dobashi Gallery in Kyoto, the first of a series of solo shows in the Kansai region. He also received major awards at the Kyoto Prefectural Art Exhibition in 1977 and 1978.

During the middle of the 1960's, Ushio Gallery in Kyoto began representing Higashi's work. This relationship would continue until 1976, when the gallery closed. In the early 1970's, an artist by the name of Noguchi Ramposai came to Higashi to seek his advice and design ideas, and they met once a week for about year. Higashi was pleased with Noguchi's progress and introduced him to Ushio Gallery, which began showing the work of both artists. During one of his many visits to Kyoto, Lloyd Cotsen happened to visit Ushio Gallery where he saw a piece of Noguchi's work and purchased it. Cotsen was very excited by the visual power and beauty of the basket and decided that on a future visit to Kyoto, he wanted to visit the artist. Mary Kahlenberg, who was a curator at Los Angeles County Museum of Art and working on a book in Japan at the time, assisted Cotsen in finding Noguchi. However, Noguchi felt it was more appropriate that Cotsen meet Higashi. This meeting led to a relationship that has continued over a quarter of a century and forms an important cornerstone of the Cotsen bamboo basket collection.

In 1979, there was a political schism in the Nitten world that led to a group of artists breaking away from the Gendai Kogei and forming the Shin Kogei. Tanabe Chikuunsai II was one of the leaders of this splinter organization. Since Tanabe was the senior bamboo artist in the Kansai region, bamboo artists including Higashi were obliged to follow him. Higashi, who always disliked politics, regretted this schism in the already small world of bamboo artists.

In the early 1980's, Higashi's youngest son, Masahiko, attended school in the United States, which led to the first of three visits by Higashi. The family visited New York City, Washington DC, and Niagara Falls. He was amazed by the vastness of the country. Masahiko's career in environmental science led to many trips to universities around the United States.

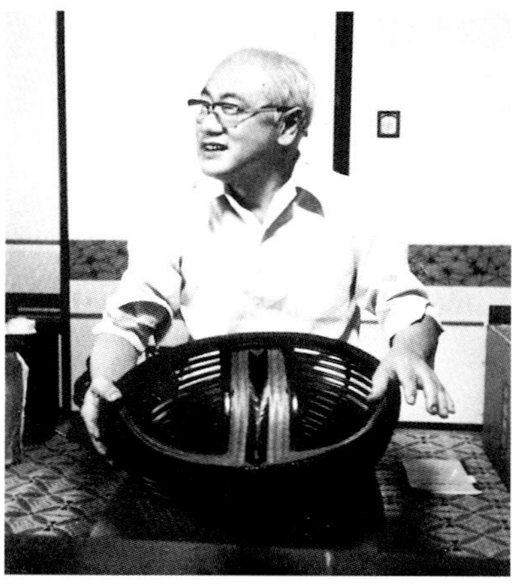

1978, Higashi showing his work to Mr. Cotsen

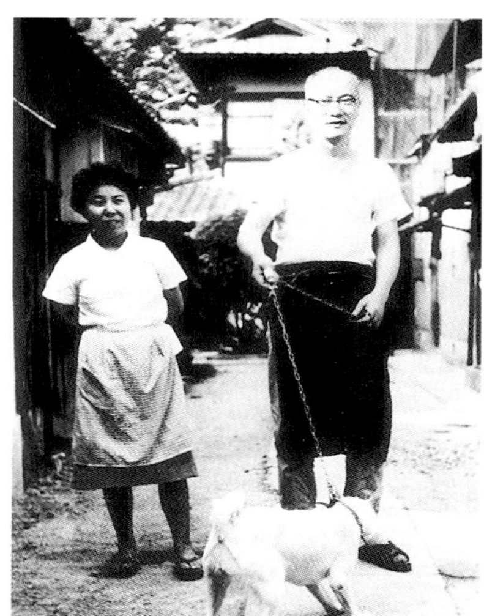

1980, Higashi and his wife, Toshie

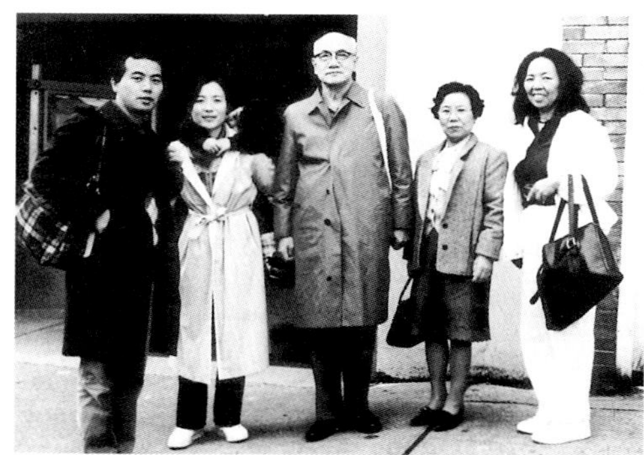

1988, Higashi in Seattle for solo exhibition Pictured: His son Masahiko and his wife Tomoko, Higashi, his wife Toshie, and interpreter

During a visit to Seattle, he was introduced to the director of the Asian Art Museum. This led to a solo show of Higashi's work in 1988. He was deeply touched that his son would help to make this happen, and that his work could be seen and enjoyed by people in America.

Higashi continued to experiment in new forms through the 1980s as shown in "Morning Fog" with its twisted strands of bamboo, "Window" with its inverted usage of the stacked and splayed bamboo at the top, and "Wave" with its lyrical sweeps of overlapping bamboo (Figure 11). But like many senior bamboo artists, he also started to revisit and further develop ideas from earlier works. The Cotsen collection has a superb example of this trend in his career with 1975's "Wave" and 1987's "Night Wave" with its beautiful usage of smoked bamboo (Figure 12). Another important event for Higashi in the middle of the 1980's was that he stopped taking orders from tea ceremony shops. His financial situation was stable enough that he could concentrate on creating only what he wanted. This new sense of freedom also led to a re-evaluation of his exhibiting in the Nitten world. He felt that work was not being properly judged, and there was too much emphasis on the sculptural quality of work and not enough on technique.

This led to his ceasing to submit to Nitten, after exhibiting for 37 years.

Instead, Higashi decided to leave and exhibit in the Dento Kogei organization, believing with its larger number of bamboo artists, Dento Kogei was the most important venue in the bamboo art world. He wanted to have his work seen by the younger generation of bamboo artists, and these artists warmly welcomed his presence. Artistically, what this meant for him was working on a smaller scale and thinking in terms of the function and tradition. An excellent example of this is the "Crossover Pattern Flower Basket" made in 1993 of smoked bamboo, and 1997's "Small Waves," which incorporated his bent bamboo technique.

In 1991, at the age of 76, Higashi developed high blood pressure and kidney problems, and began to believe that he would not live much longer. He came to peace with this possibility, and his work began to become more relaxed. At the Dento Kogei fall exhibition of 1995, Higashi won the prestigious Prince Takamatsu award. Iizuka Shokansai, the senior leader of the bamboo artists, praised the work for its quiet elegance, especially remarkable for coming from someone who had such a serious illness.

In 1997, Tai Gallery of Santa Fe New Mexico began to present Higashi's work to a wider audience in the United States and Europe. His reputation as great bamboo artist continues to grow beyond Japan. This is deeply inspiring to him and motivates him. Higashi always wants to make something new and original, and perhaps create another new technique Now his work schedule is reduced to four hours a day. It takes him about six months to complete a piece for exhibition.

When I first met Higashi, I boldly asked him if he still had the necessary strength in his hands to work with bamboo. He answered that as he grows older, his artistic vision becomes stronger. Then with a grin and twinkle in his eye, he said, "Besides, I still have about a twenty-year supply of smoked bamboo." Higashi was 82 at the time.

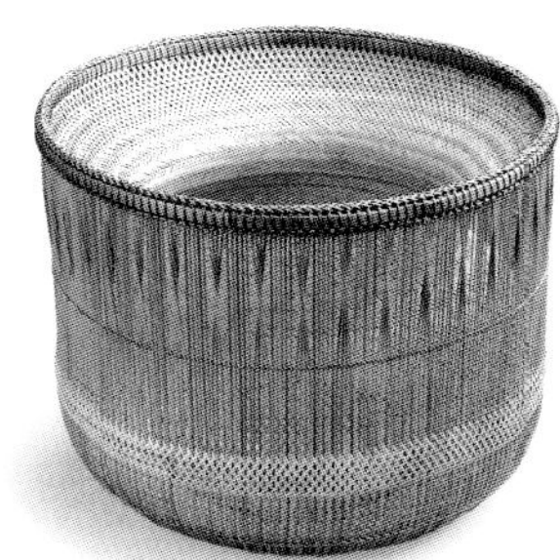

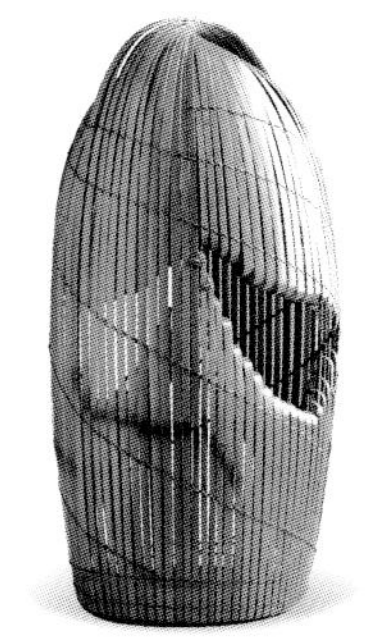

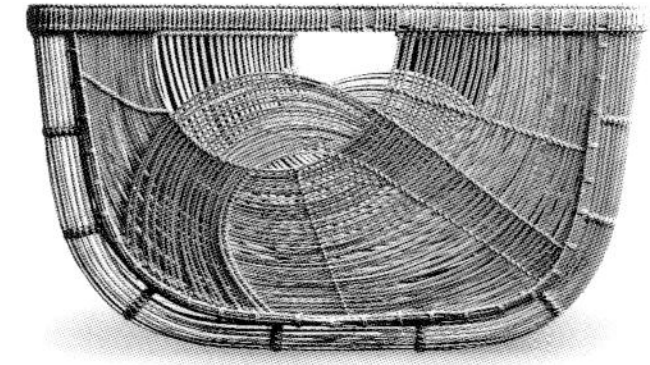

Figure 11

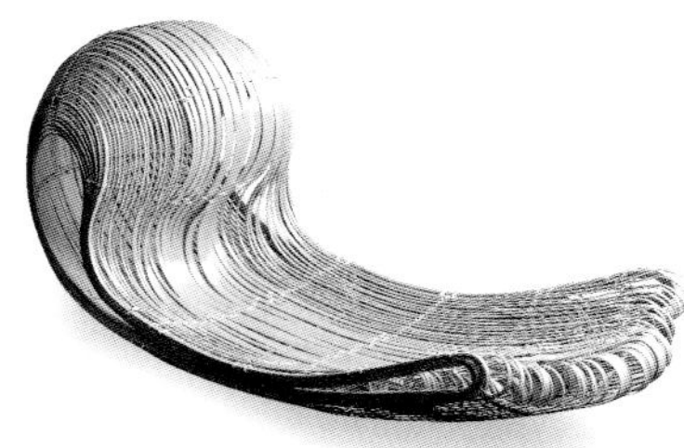

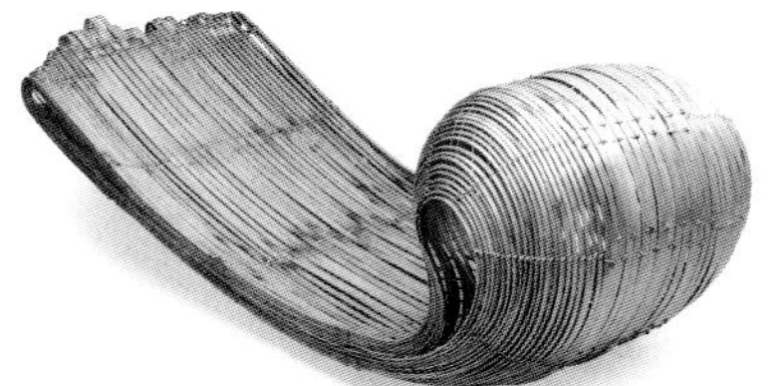

Figure 12

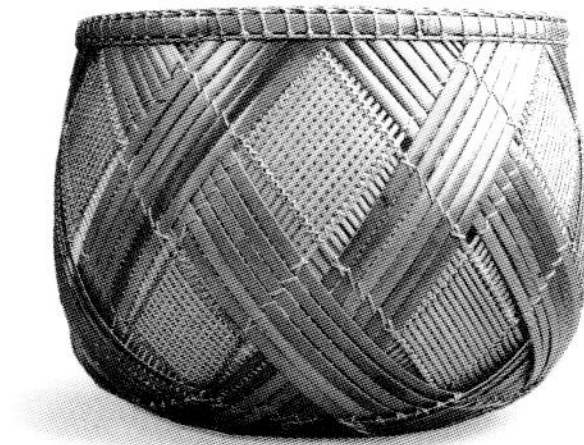

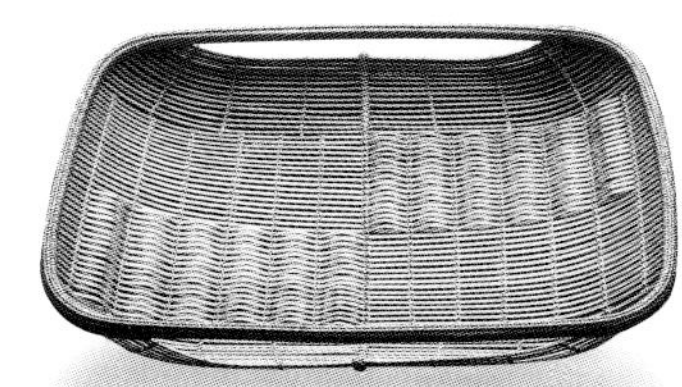

Figure 13

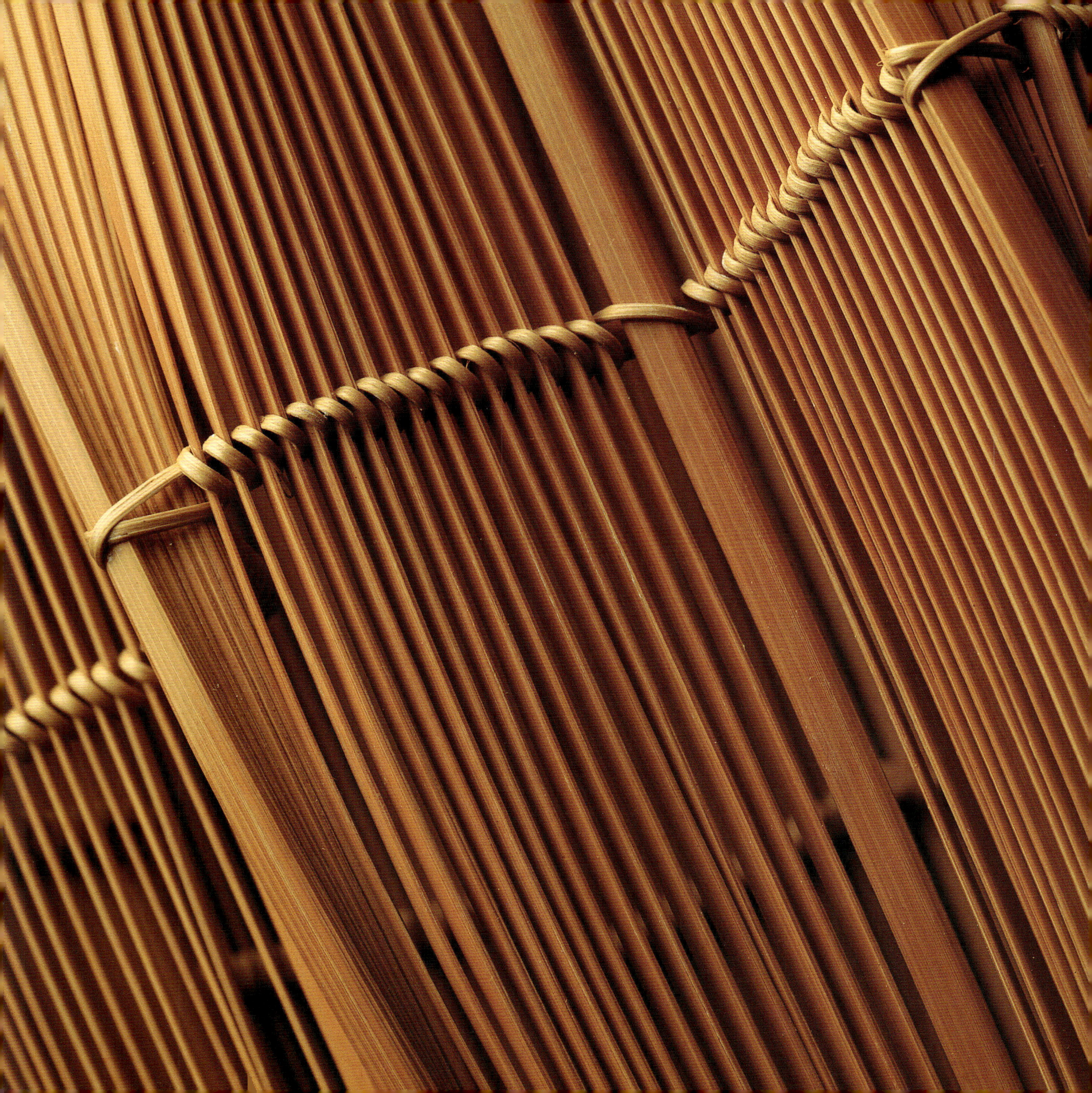

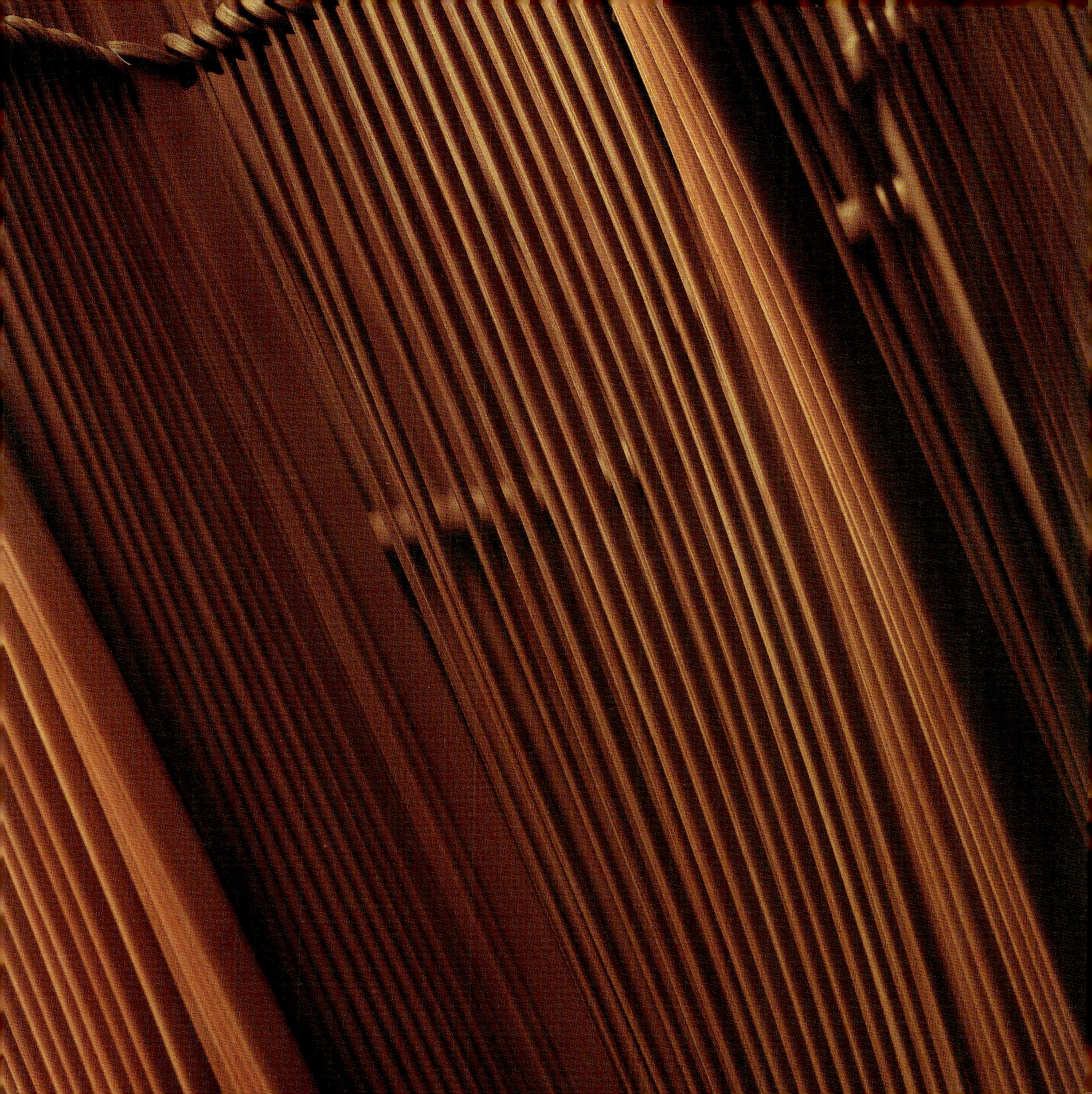

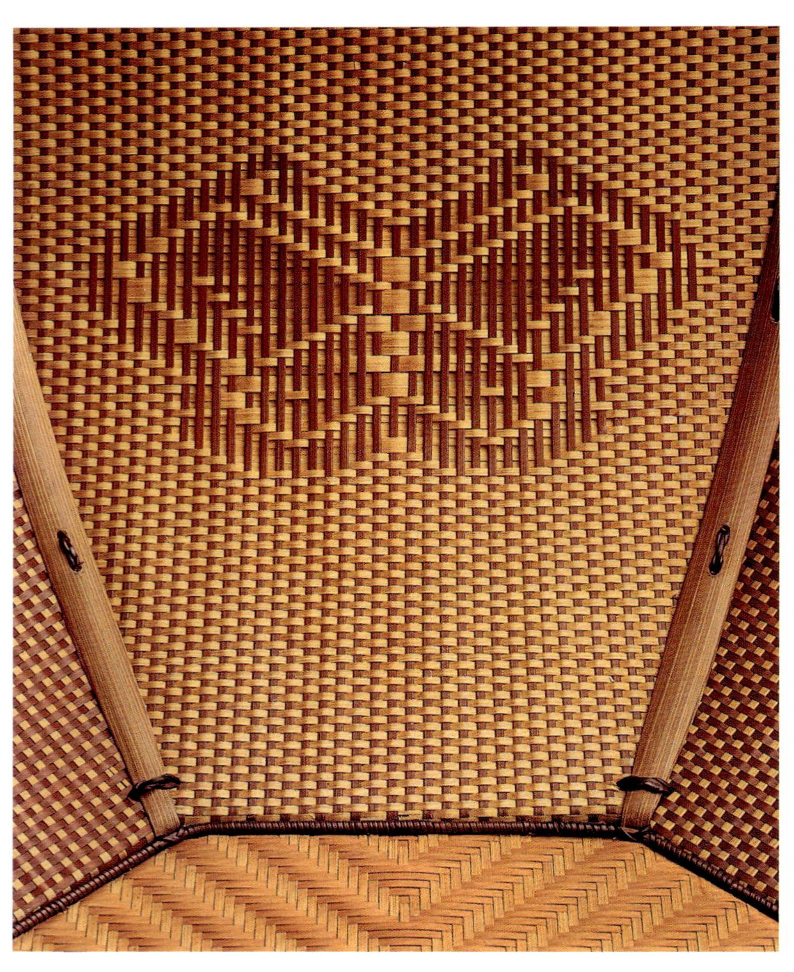

Butterfly Pattern Offering Basket

1952
26" x 26" x 9 1/2" (66 x 66 x 21cm)

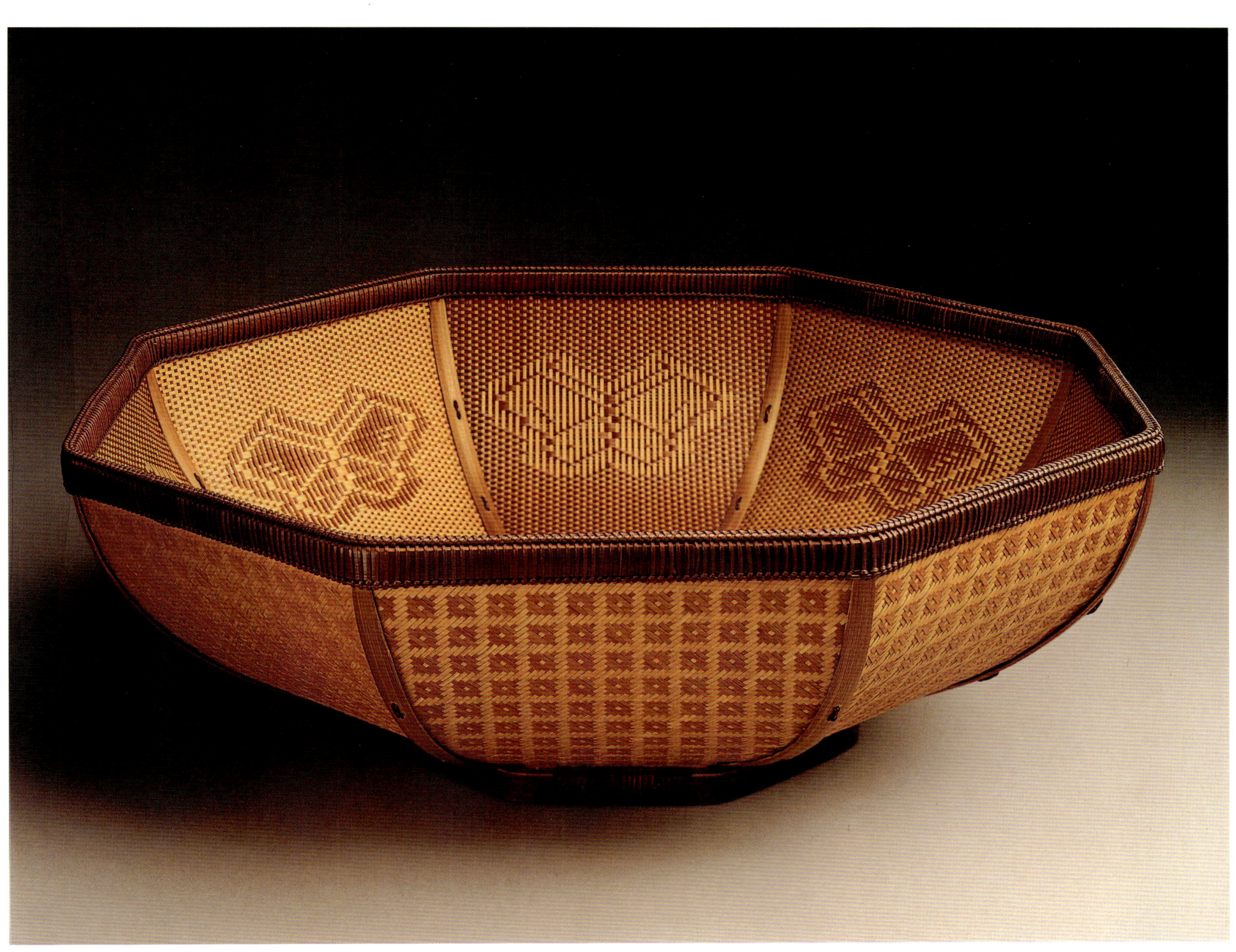

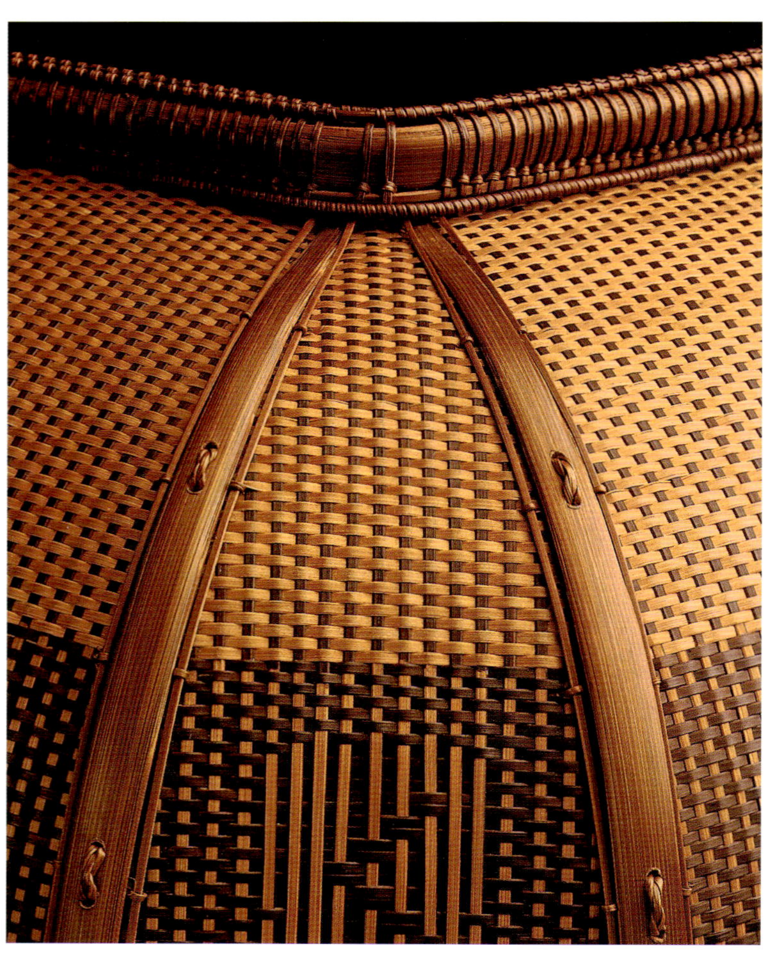

Iris Pattern Flower Basket

1954
17"x 16" x 10" (43 x 41 x 26cm)

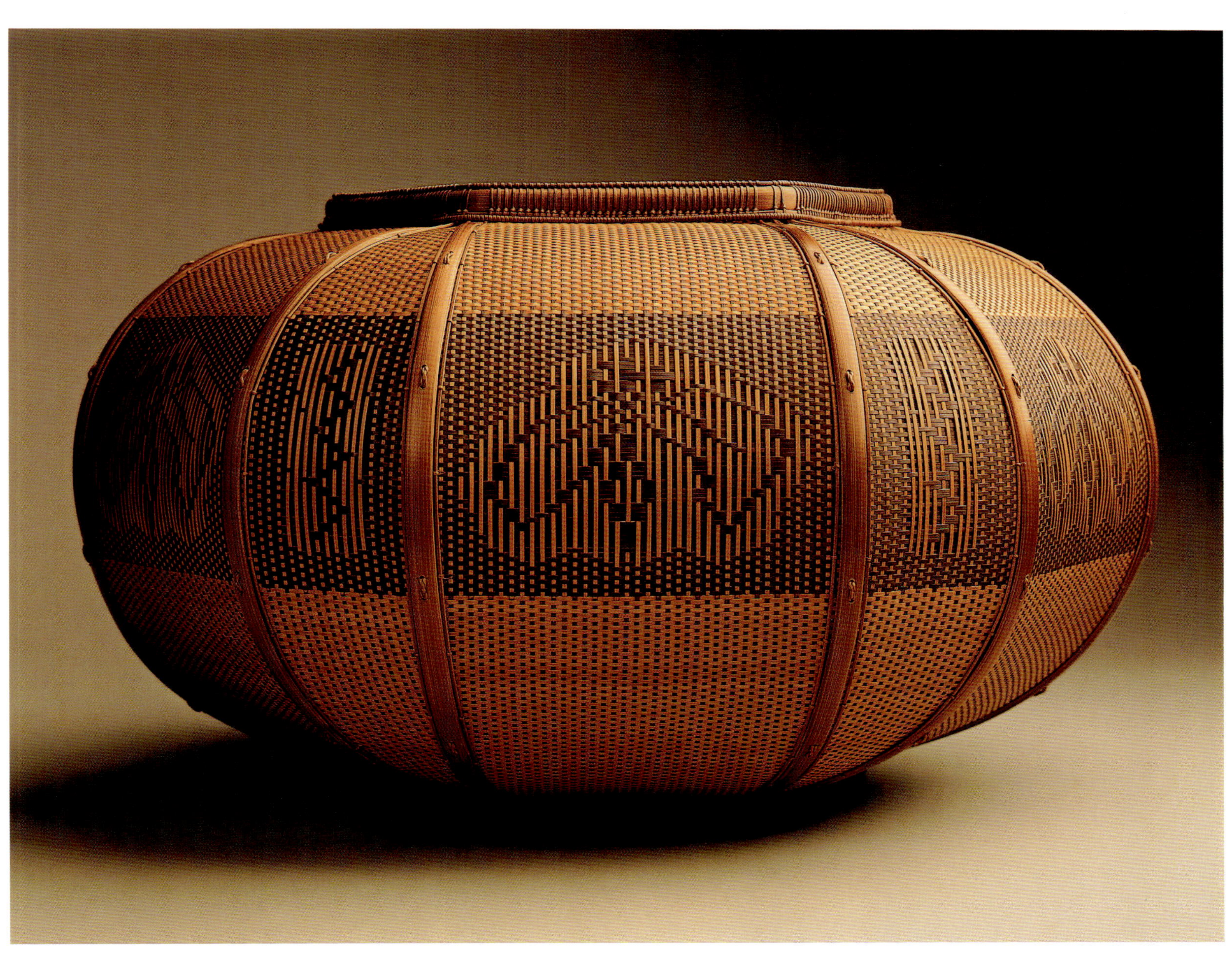

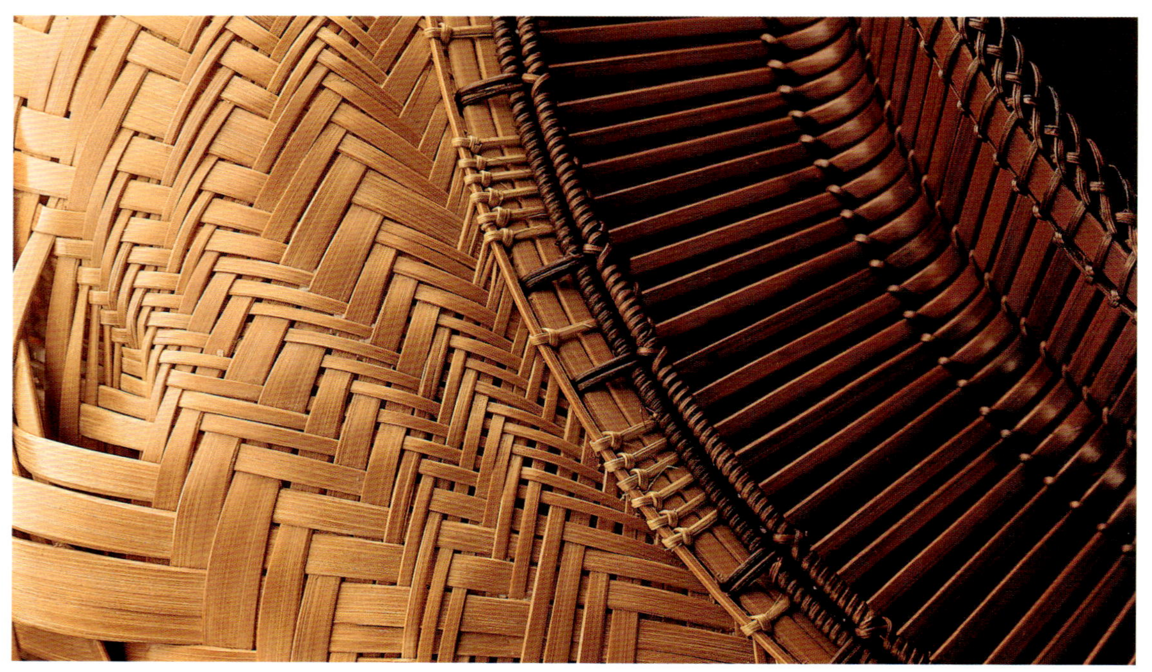

Snow Flower Pattern Flower Basket

1955
18"d x 10 1/2" (46d x 27 cm)

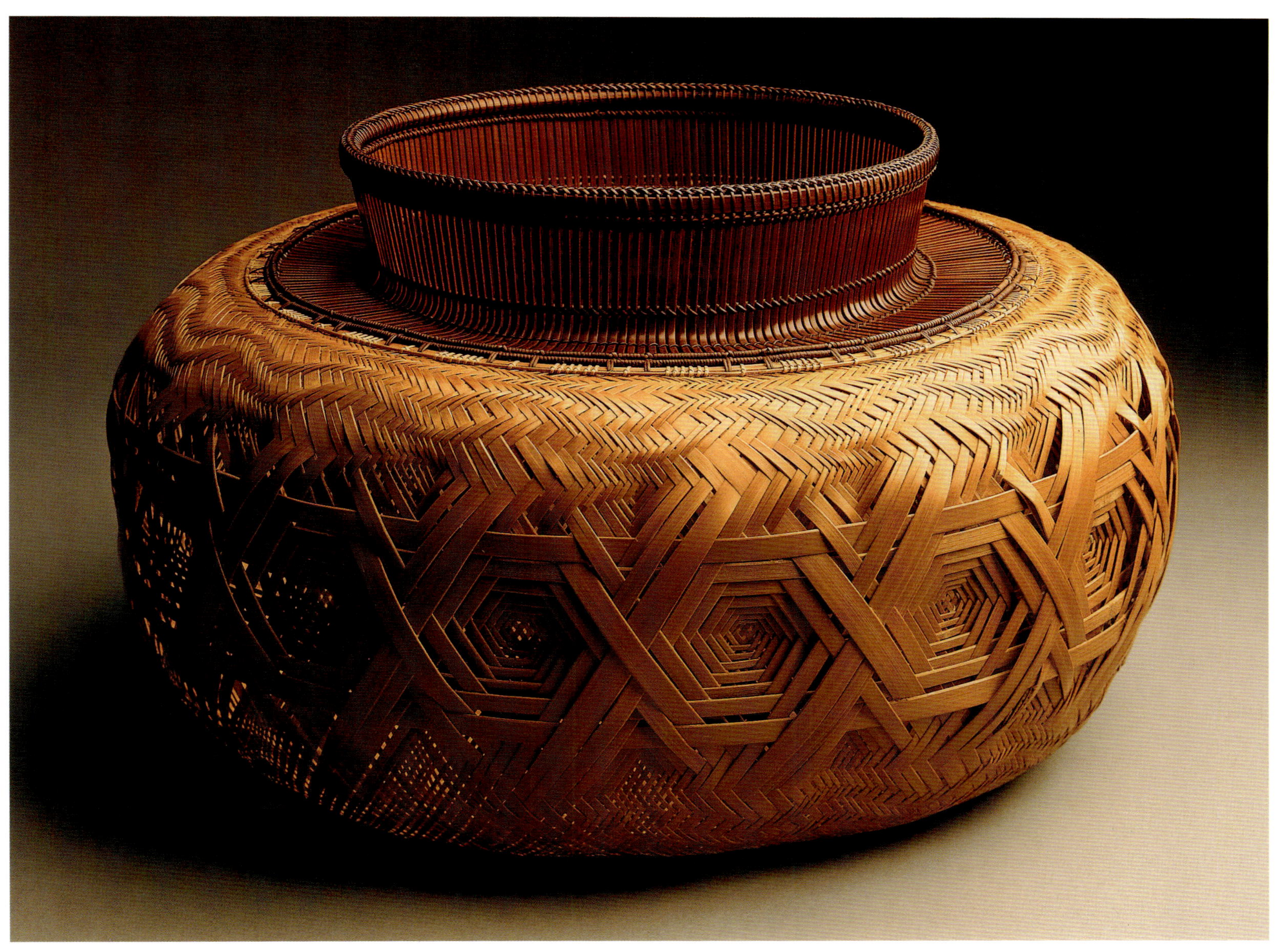

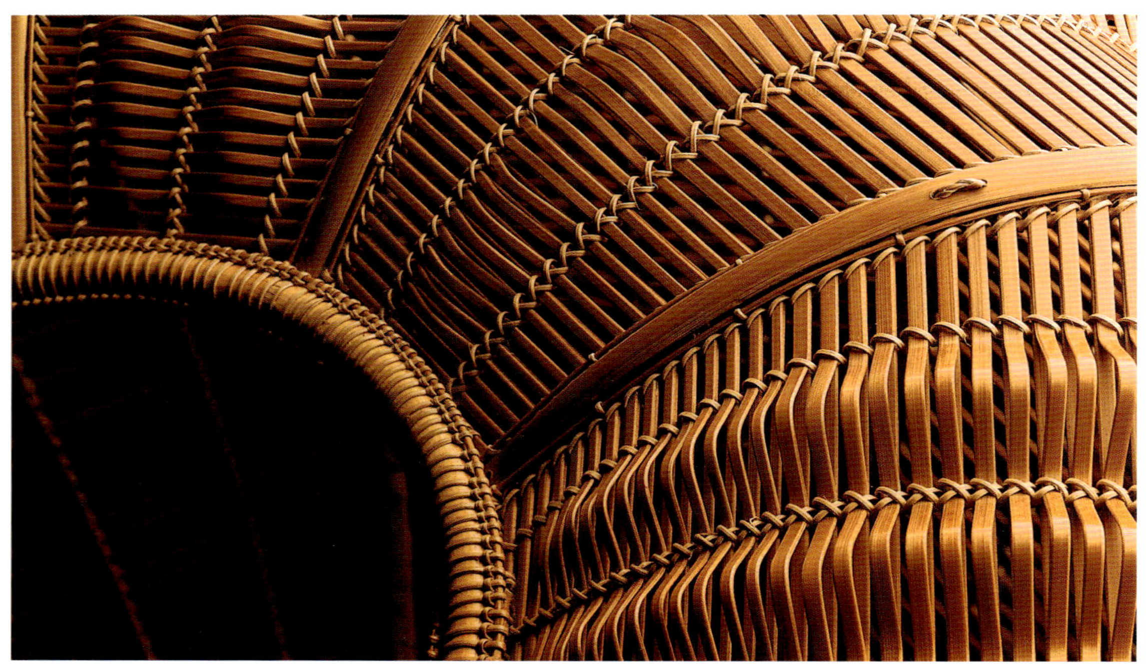

Passion Flower

1959
21"d x 11" (53d x 28 cm)

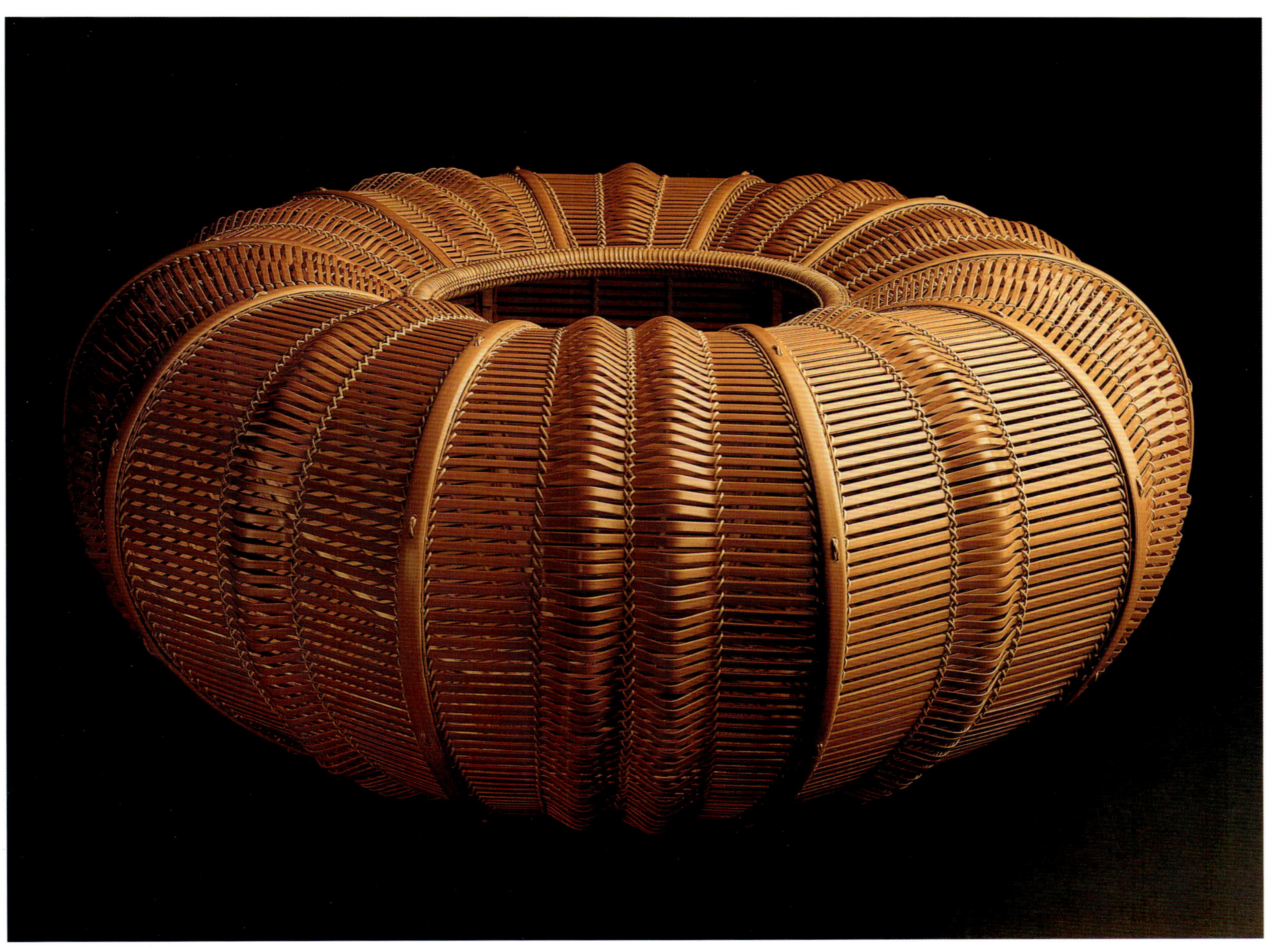

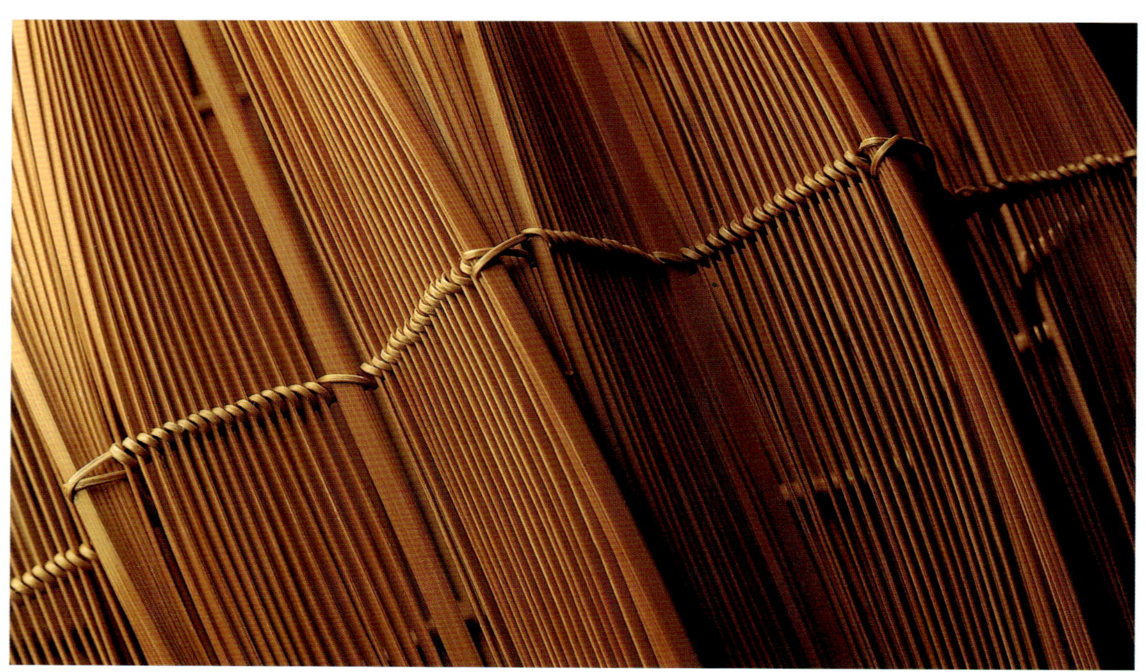

Rushing Water

1964
8"d x 14 1/2" (20d x 37 cm)

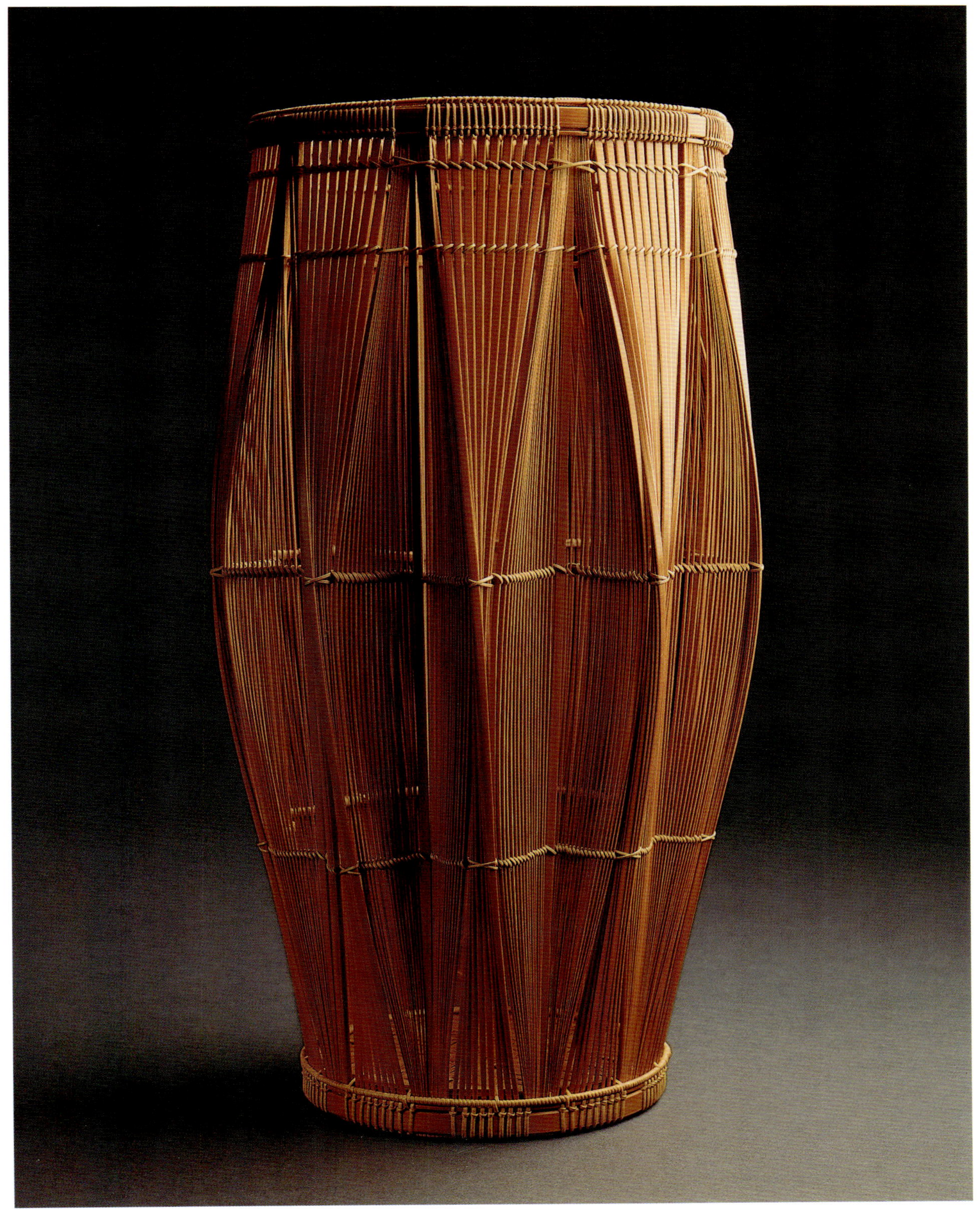

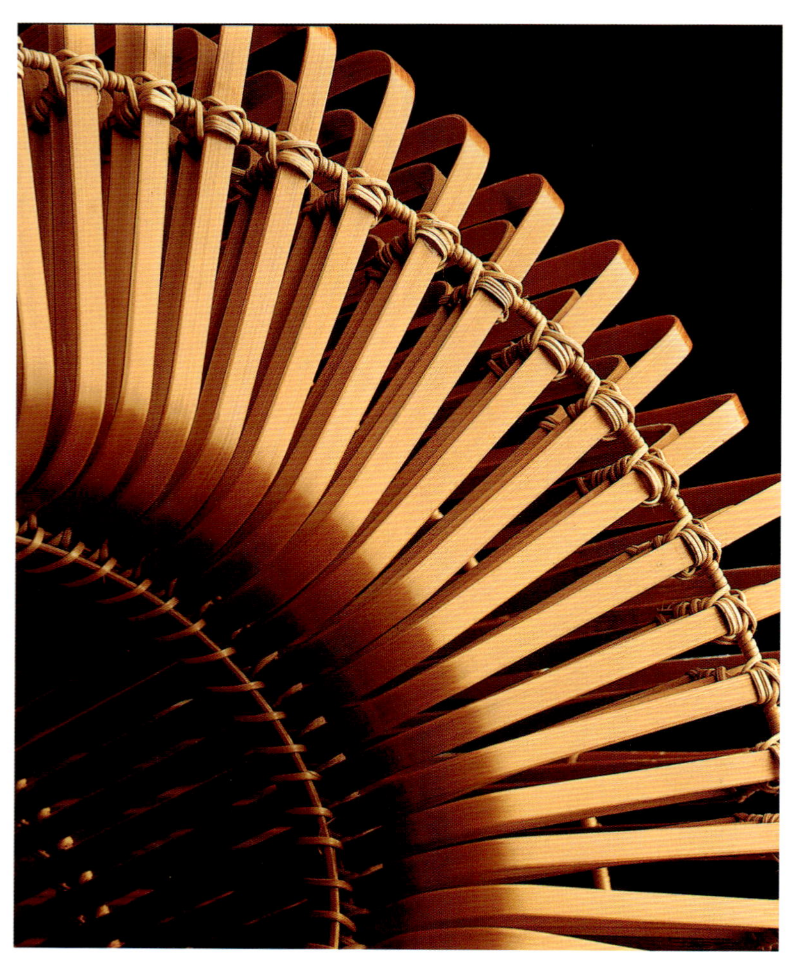

Sacred Fire

1970
12" x 15"(30 x 39 cm)

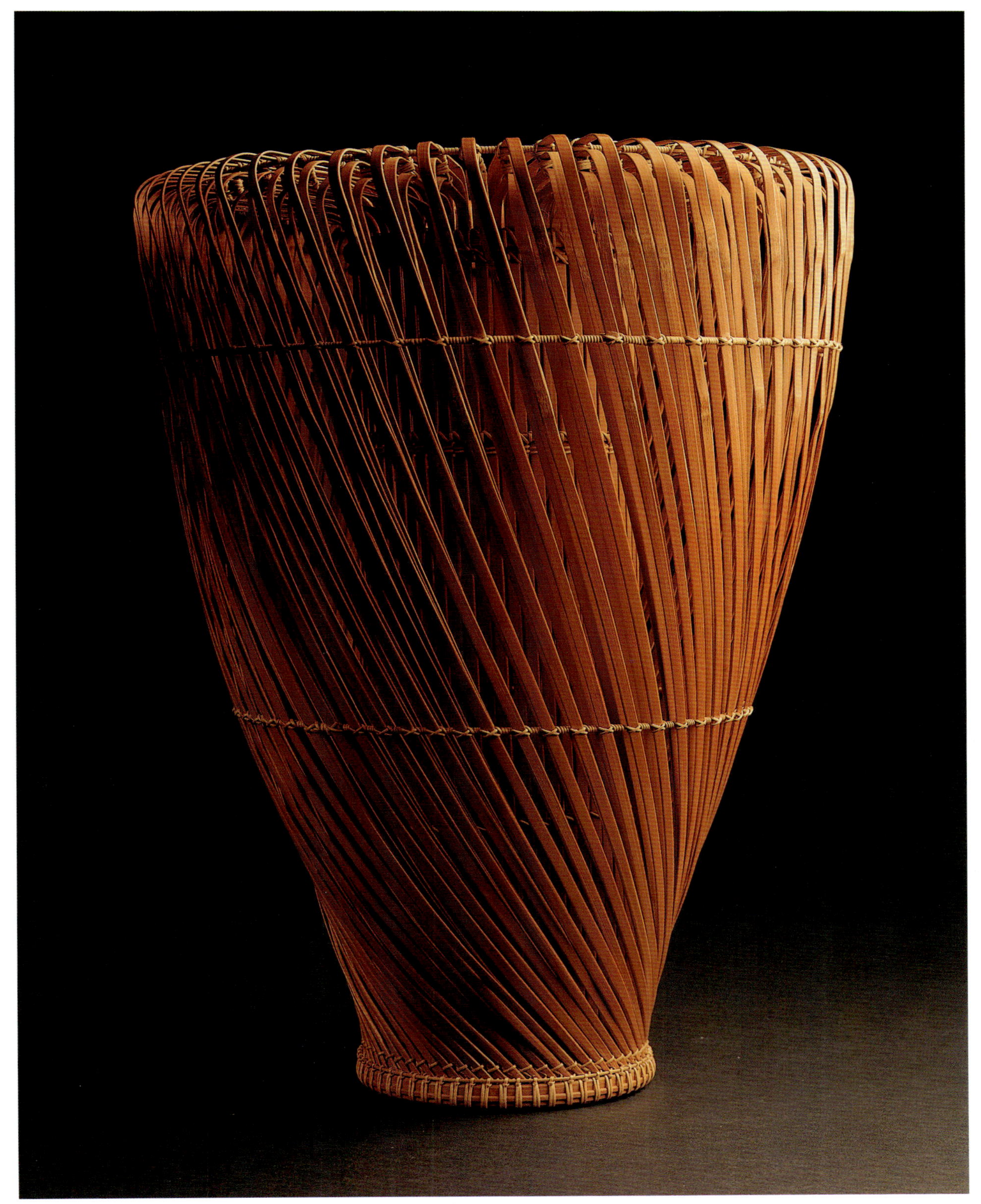

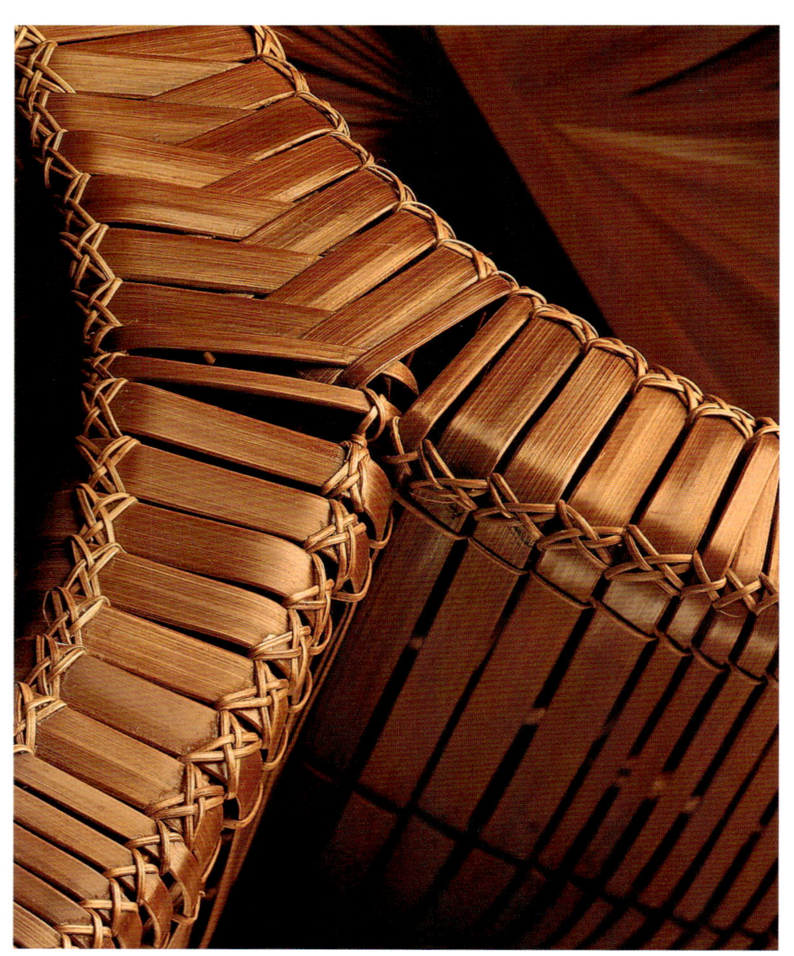

Pair

1971
27 1/2" x 24 1/2" x 9" (70 x 62 x 22 cm)

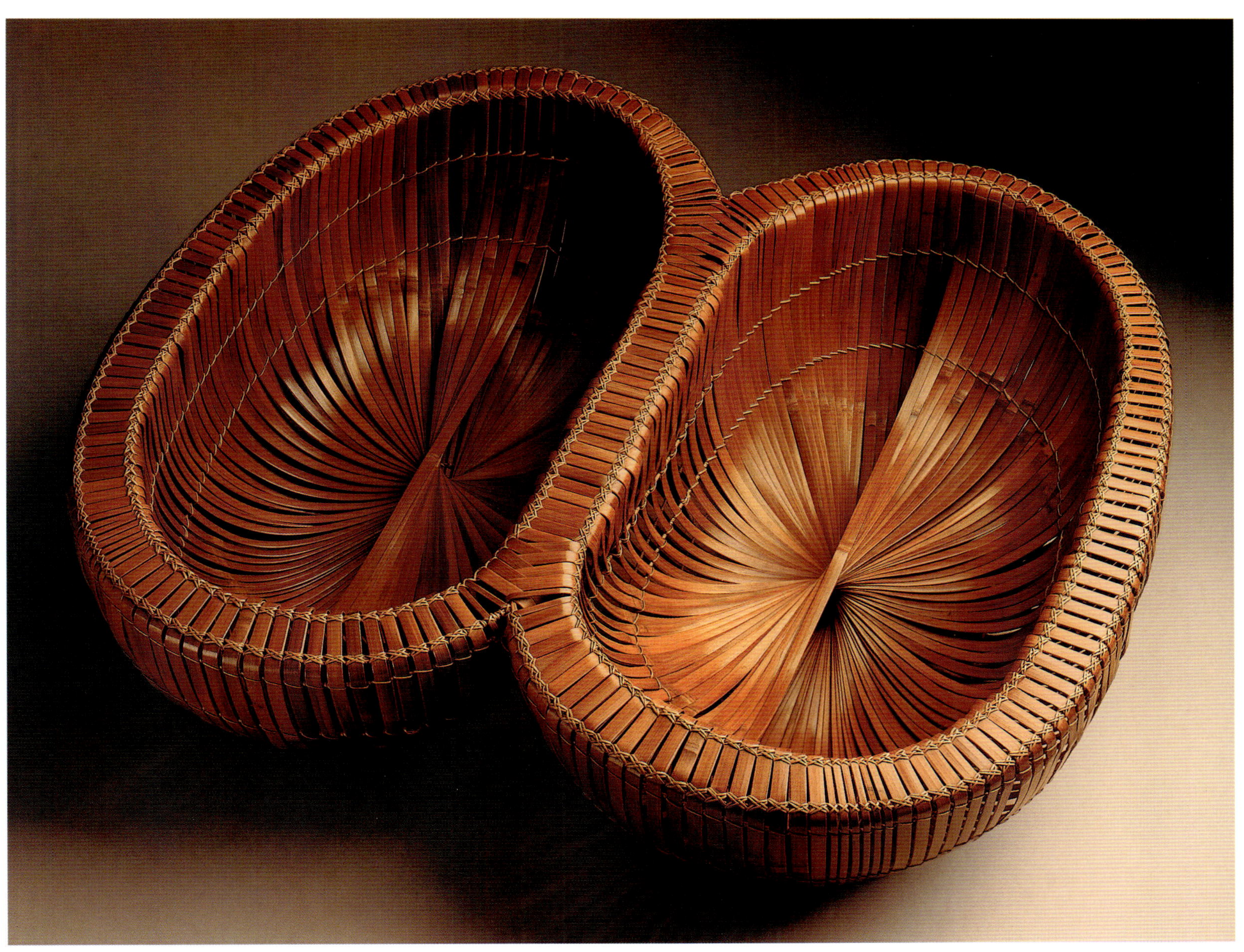

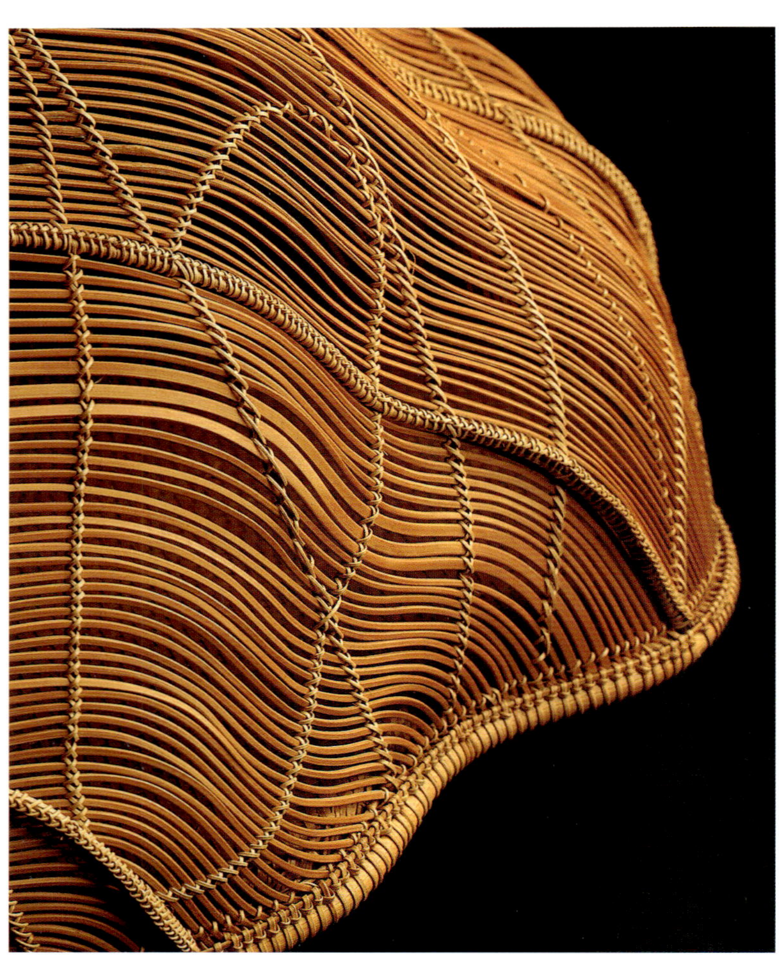

Stone in the Stream

1971
28 1/2" x 17" x 11" (72 x 43 x 28 cm)

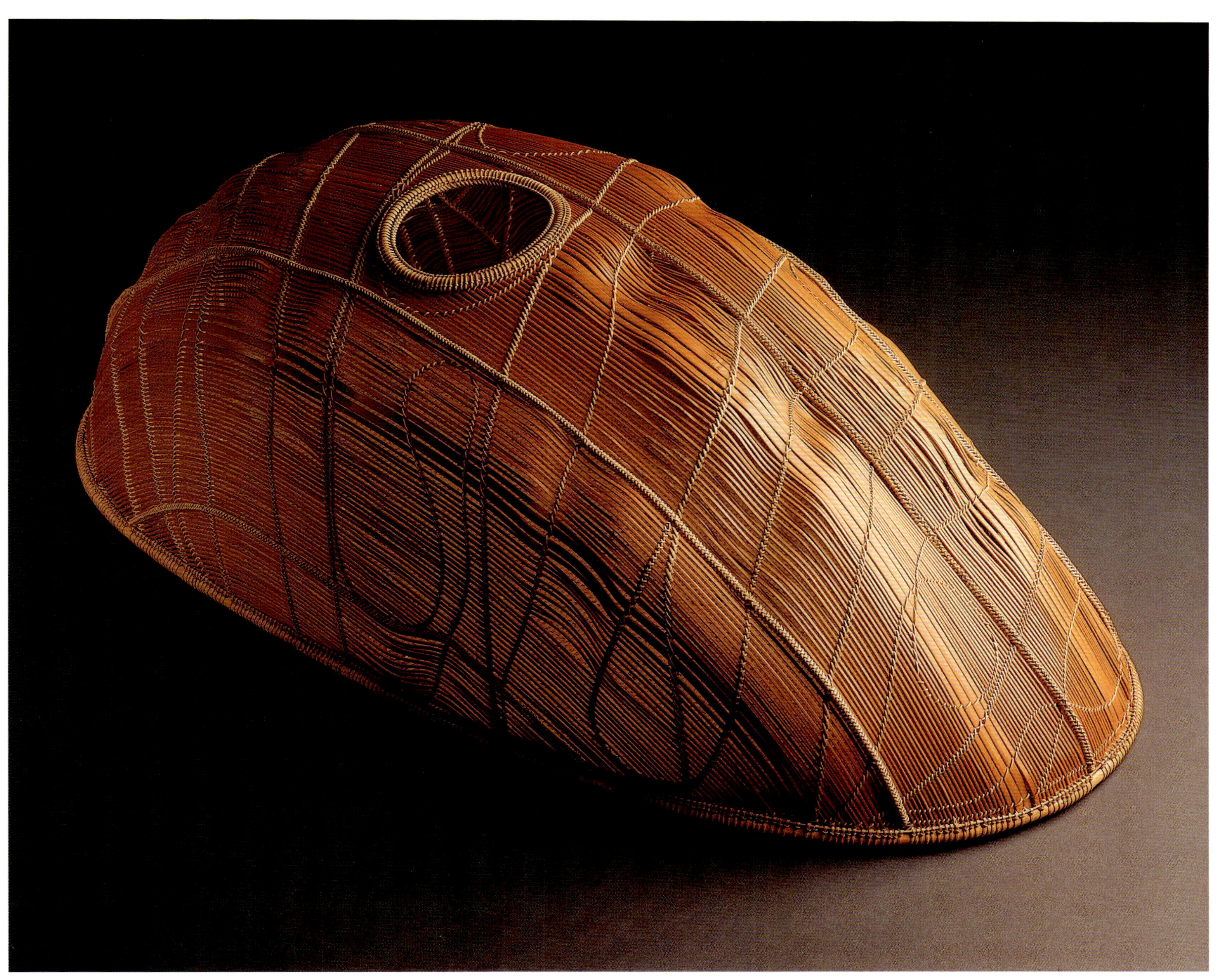

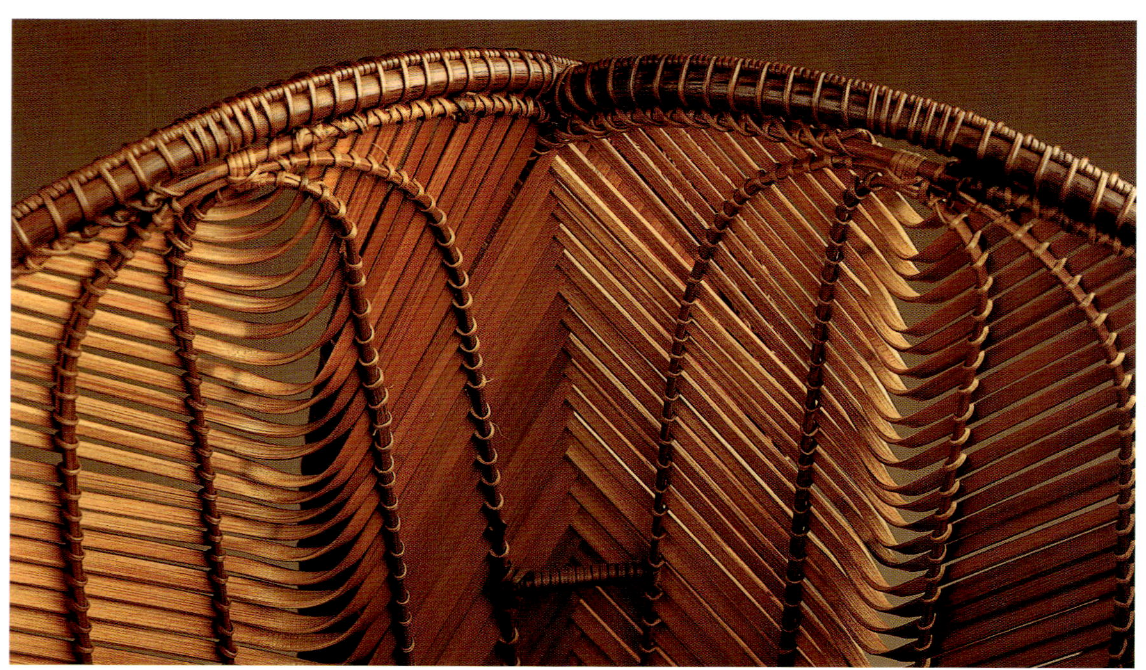

Palms Pressed Together In Prayer

1974
14" x 13" x 31" (36 x 34 x 78 cm)

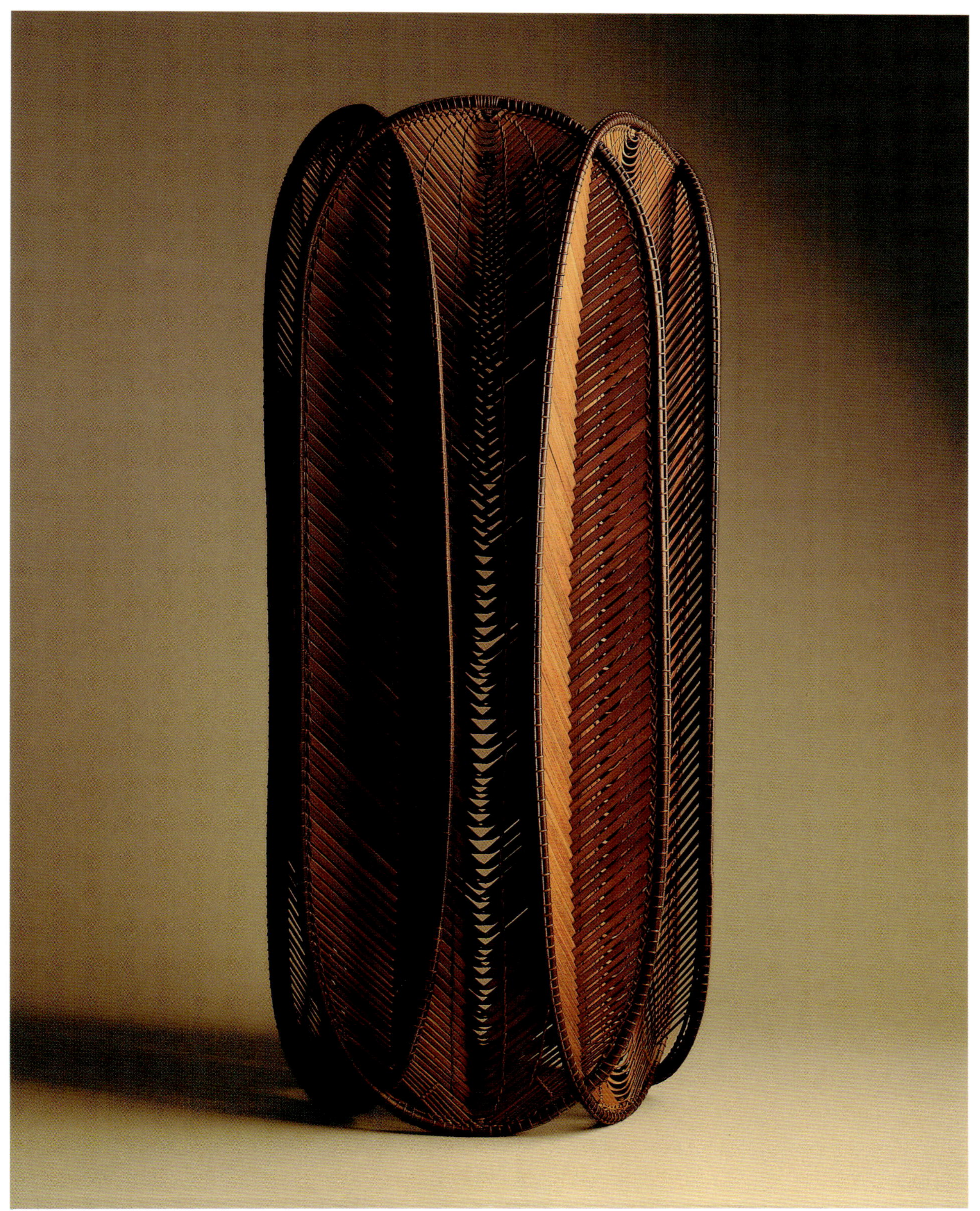

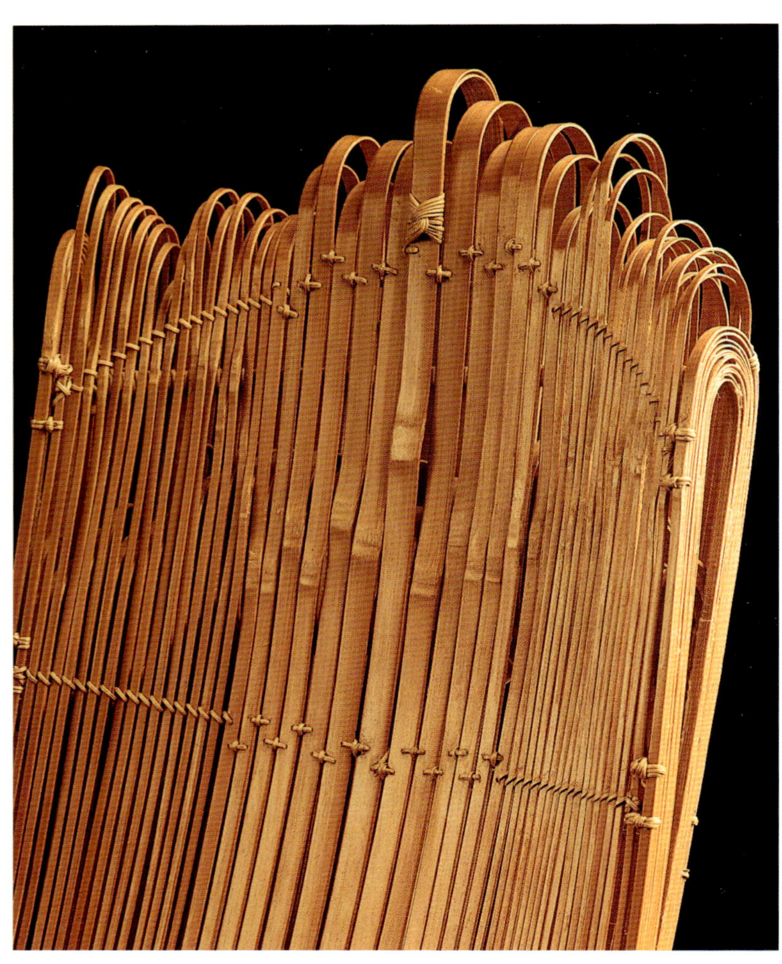

Wave

1975
25½" x 10" x 11½" (65 x 25 x 29 cm)

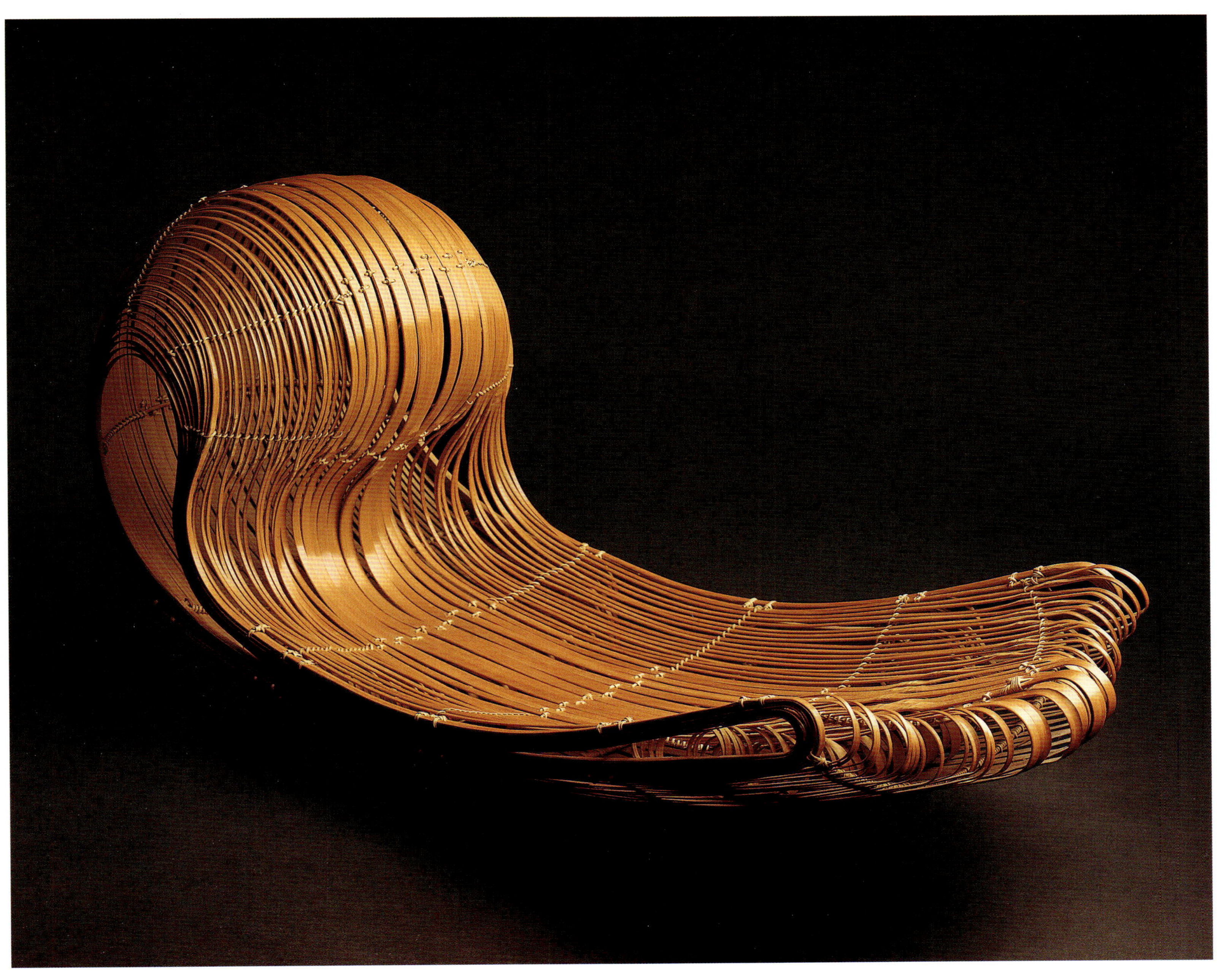

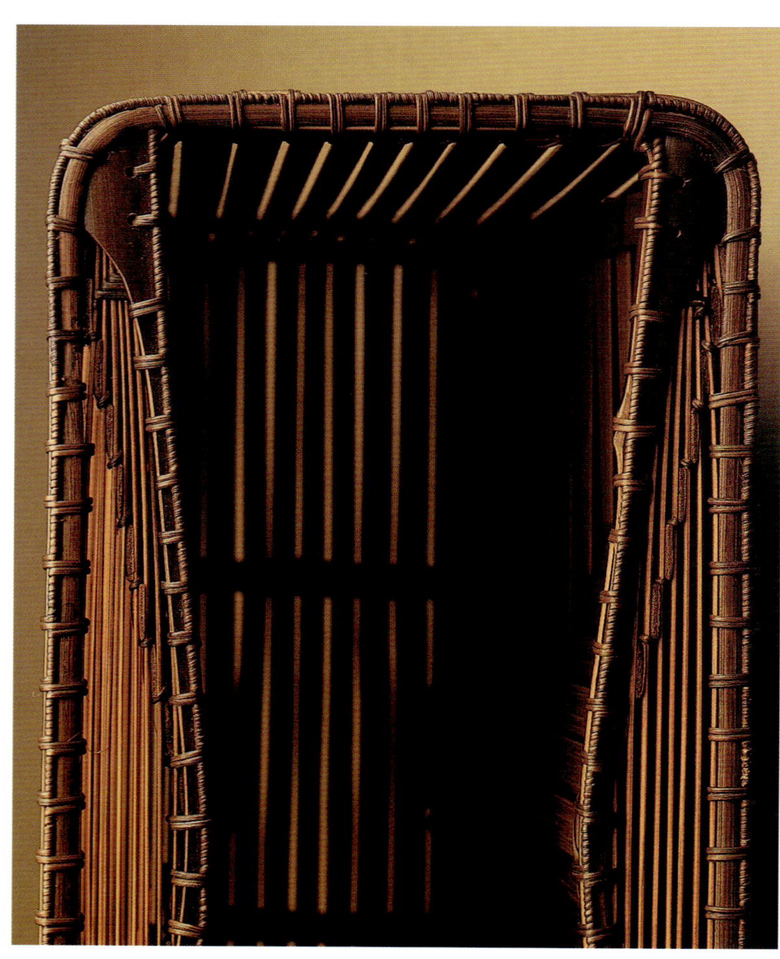

Danjuro's Crest

1975
11" x 5" x 11" (28 x 13 x 28 cm)

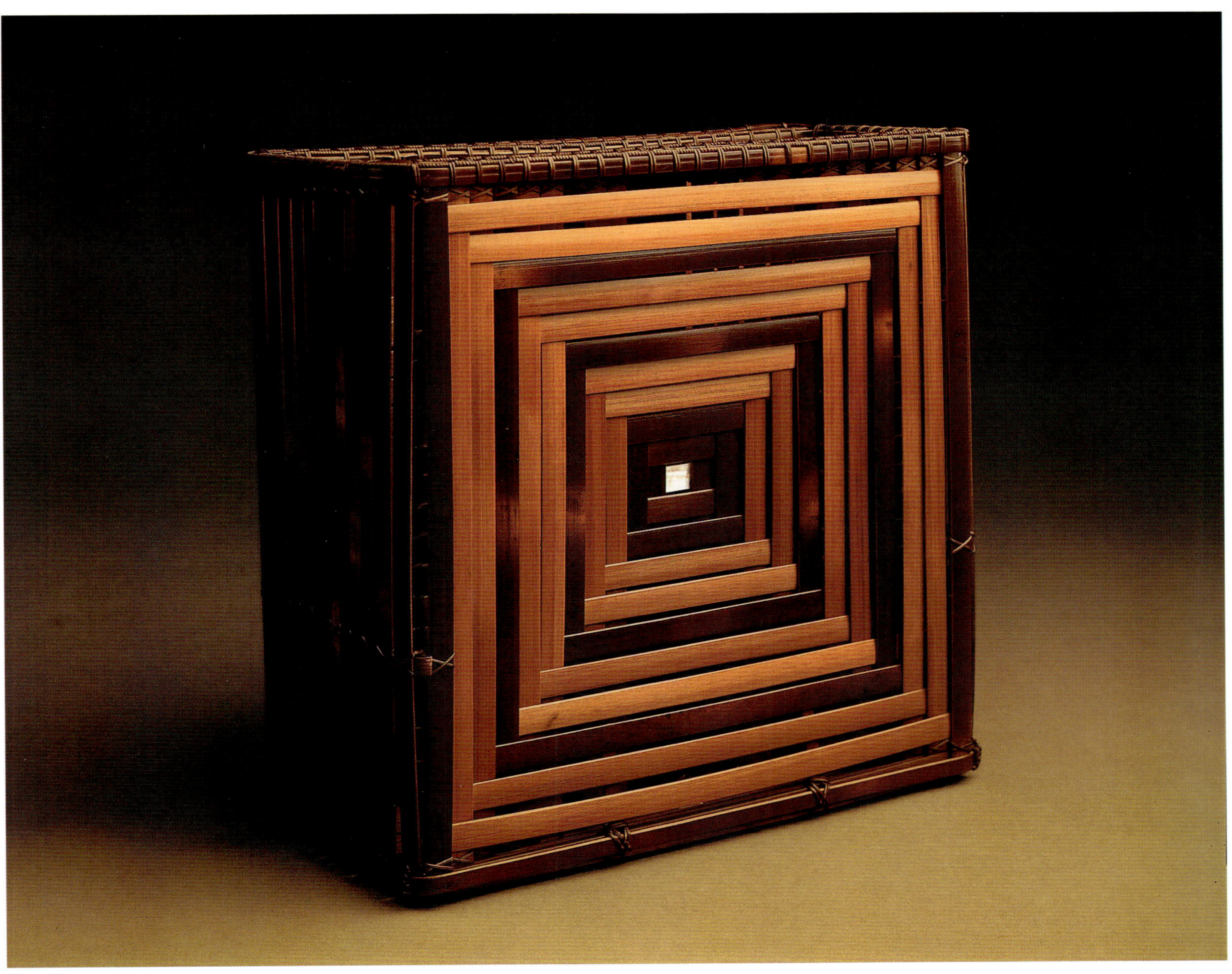

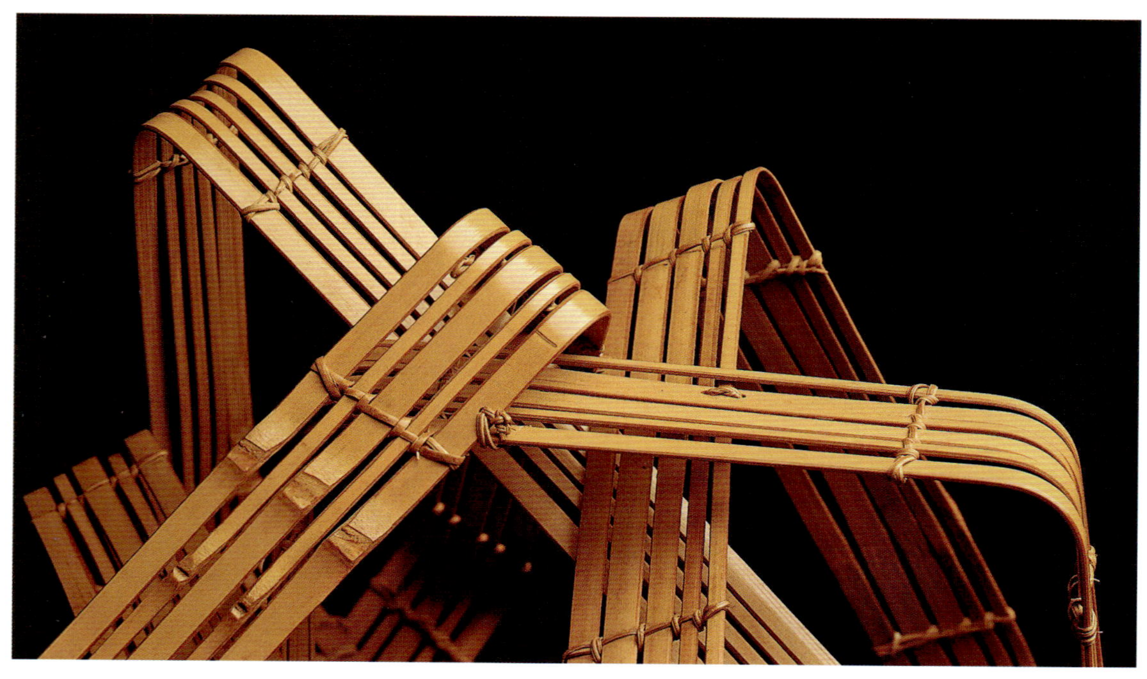

Sweet-scented Stone

1975
14" x 10" x 12" (36 x 25 x 31 cm)

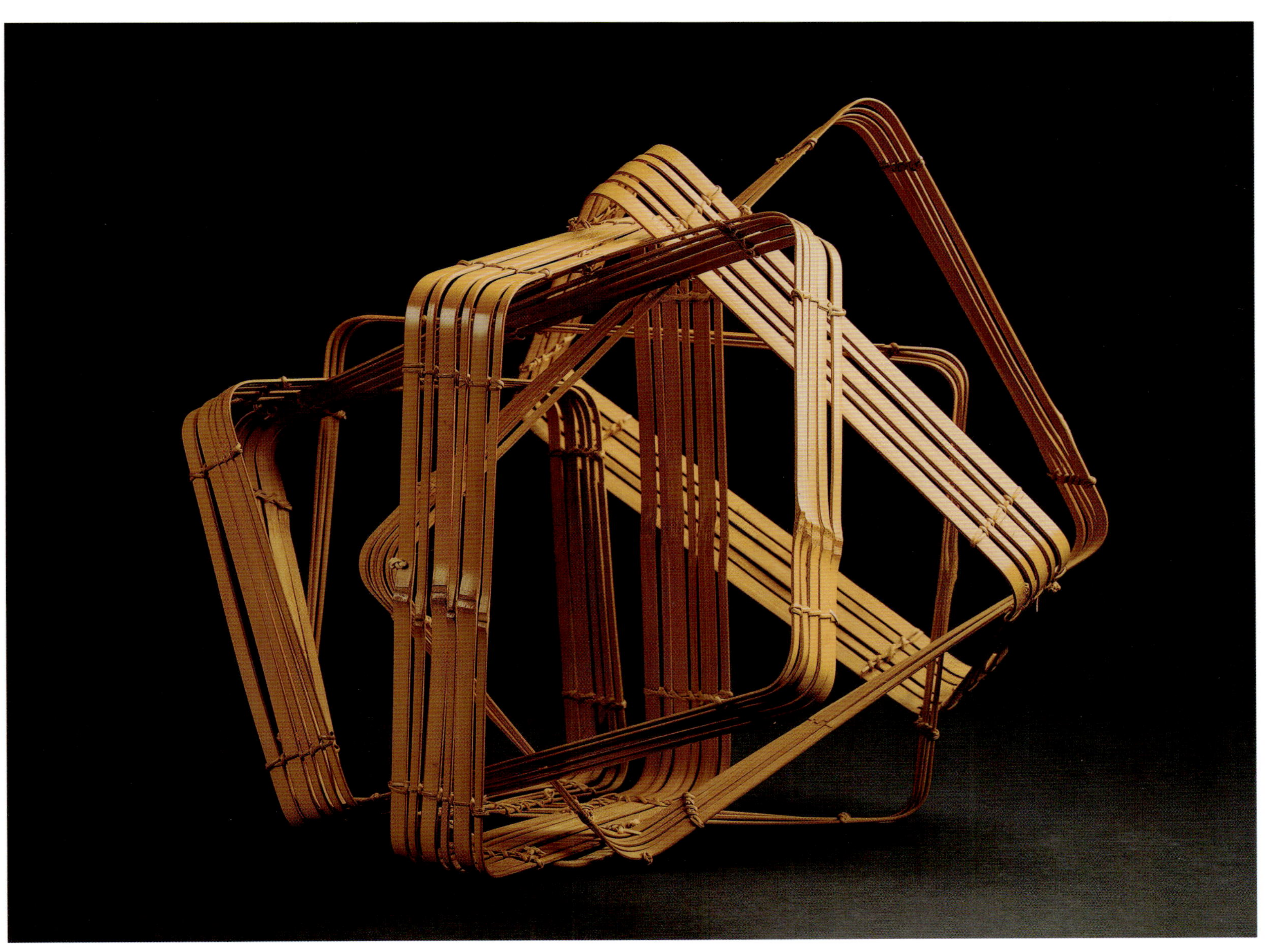

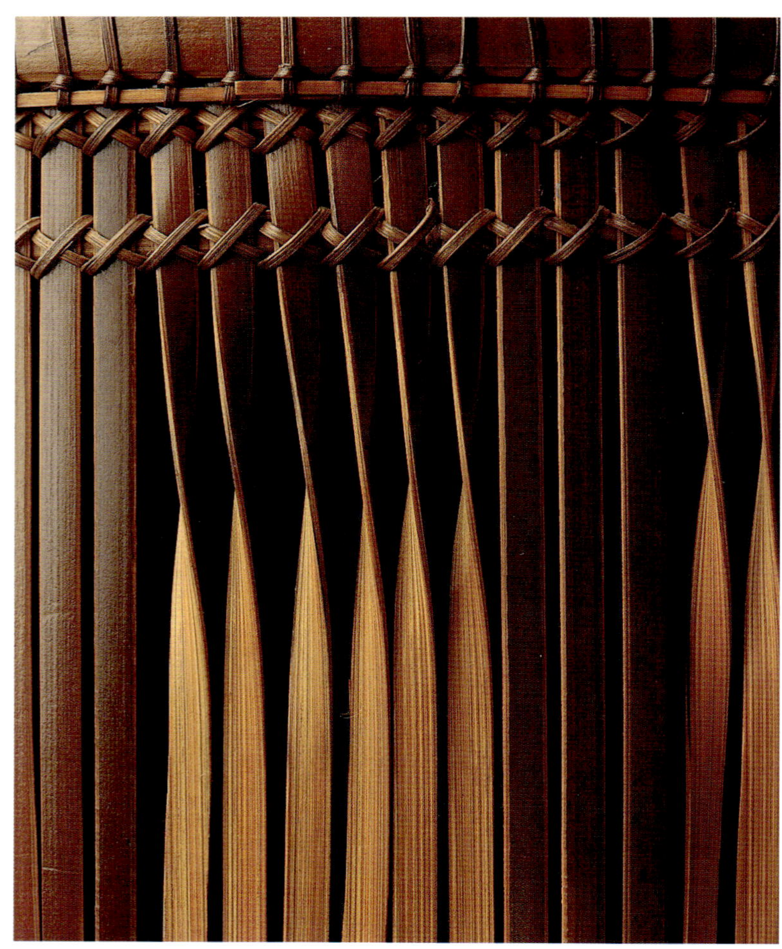

Pure Breeze

1975
7"d x 10" (18d x 25 cm)

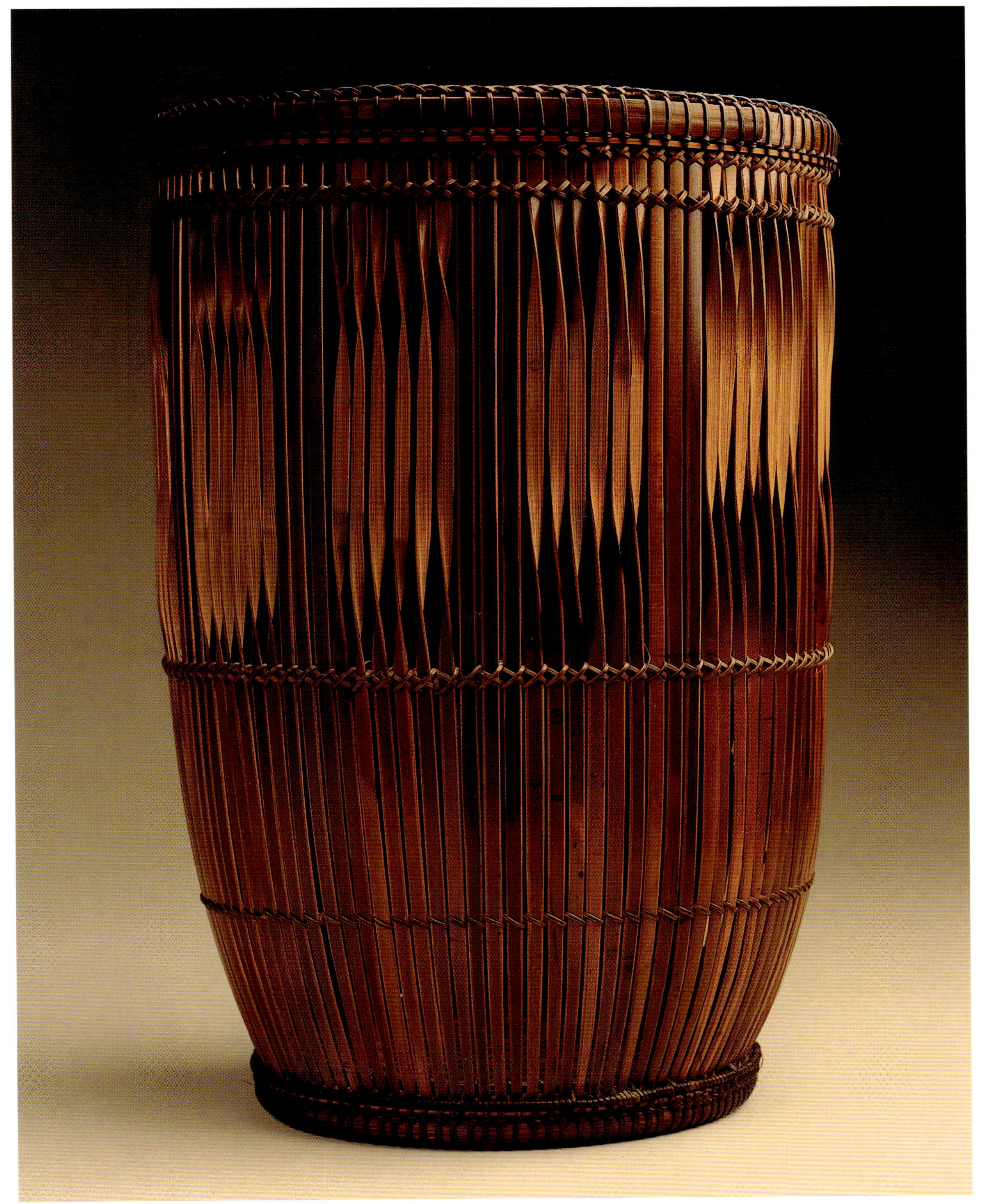

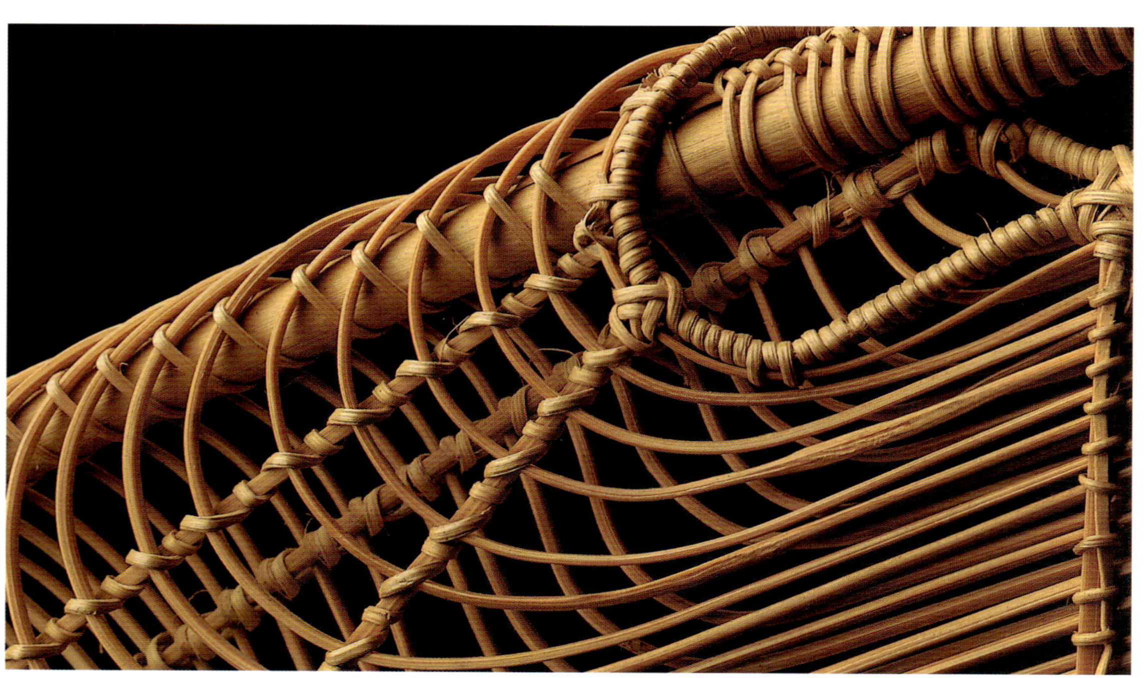

Seashore

1976
23 1/2" x 14" x 7" (60 x 36 x 18" cm)

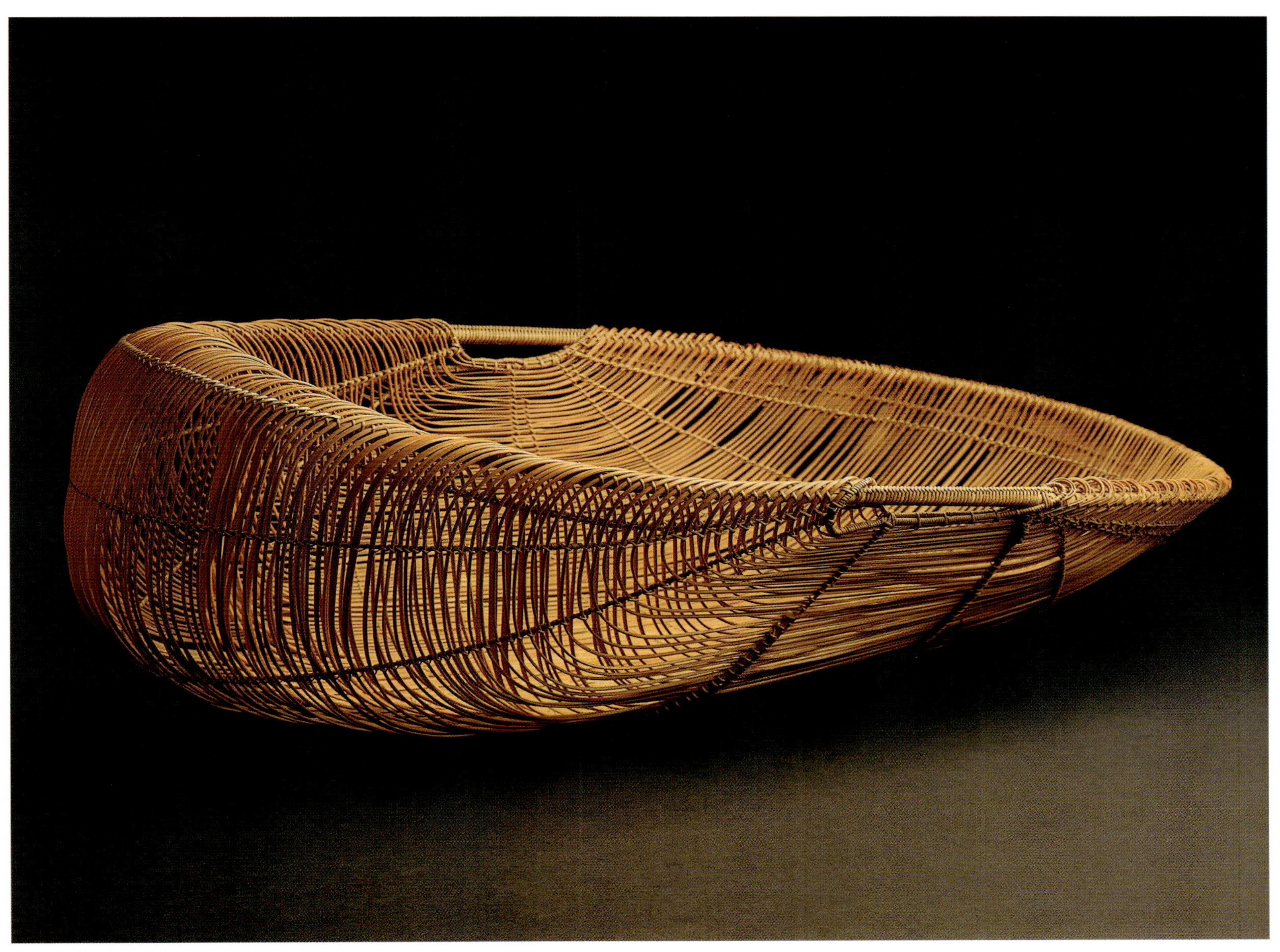

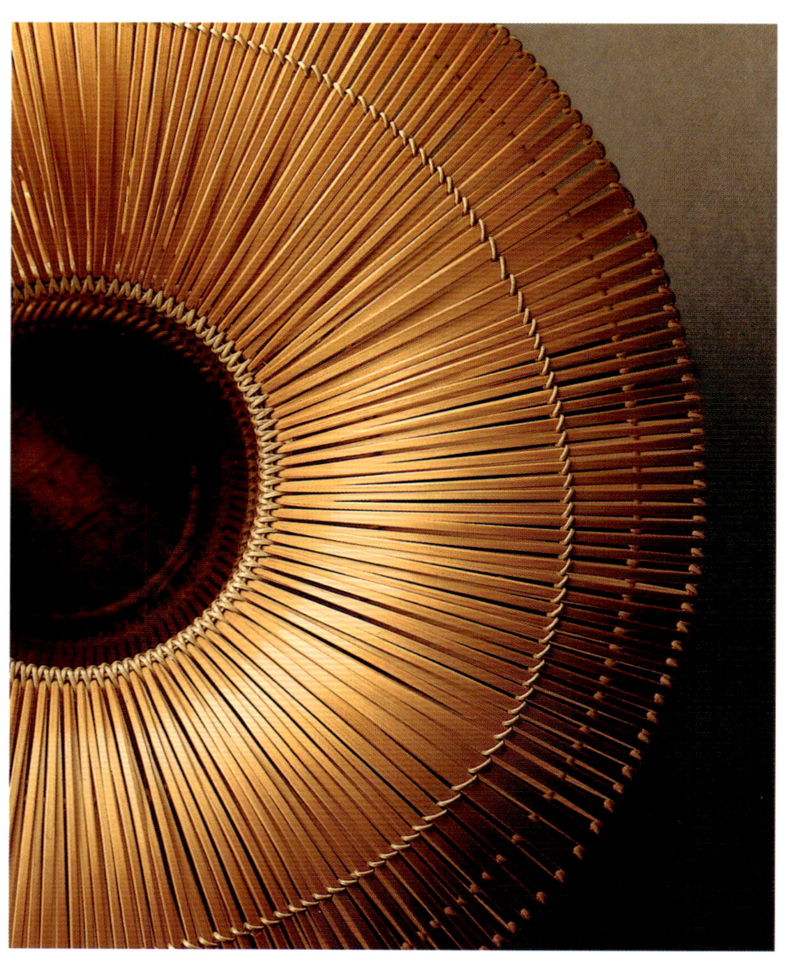

Sunlight

1976
12"d x 14" (30d x 36 cm)

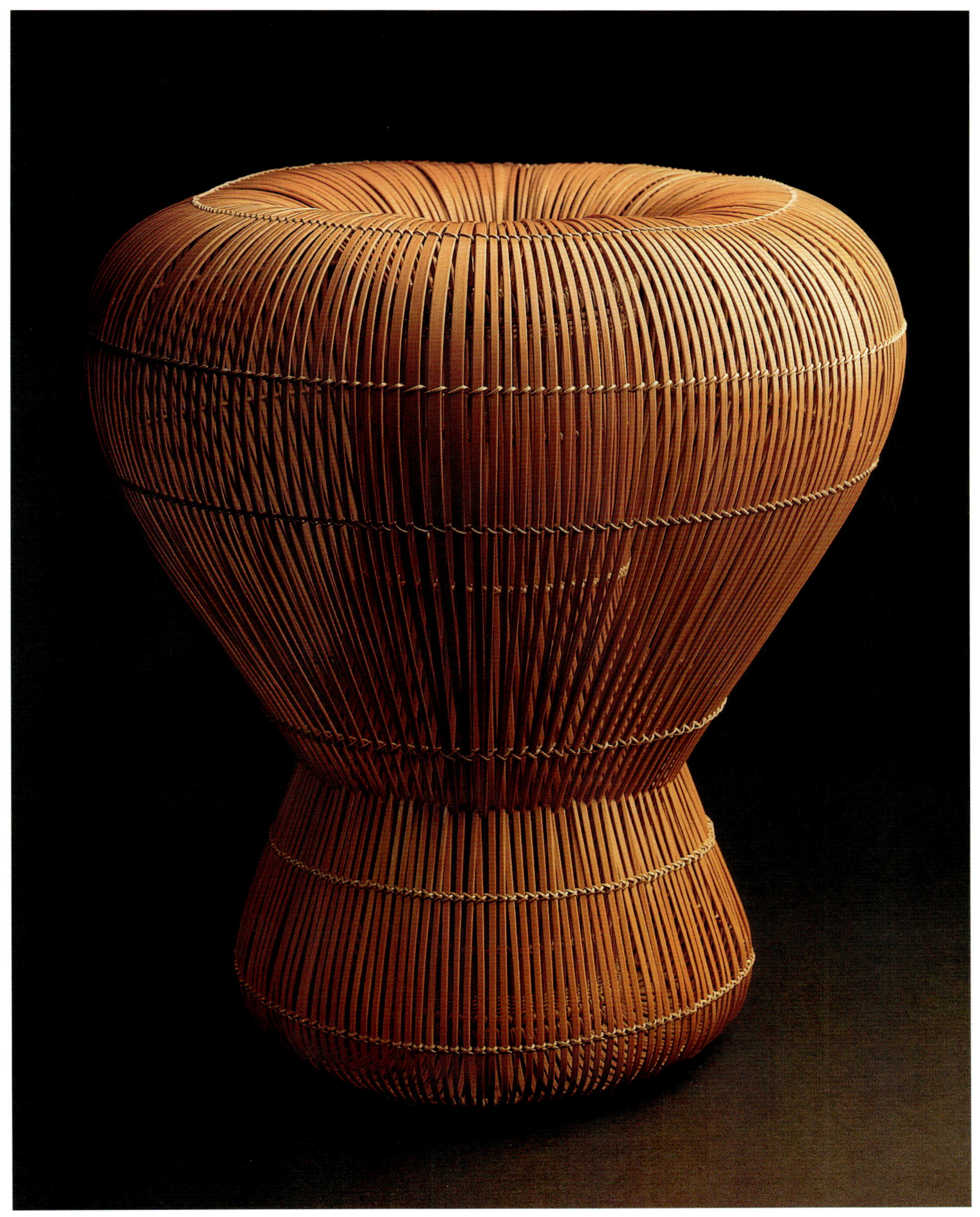

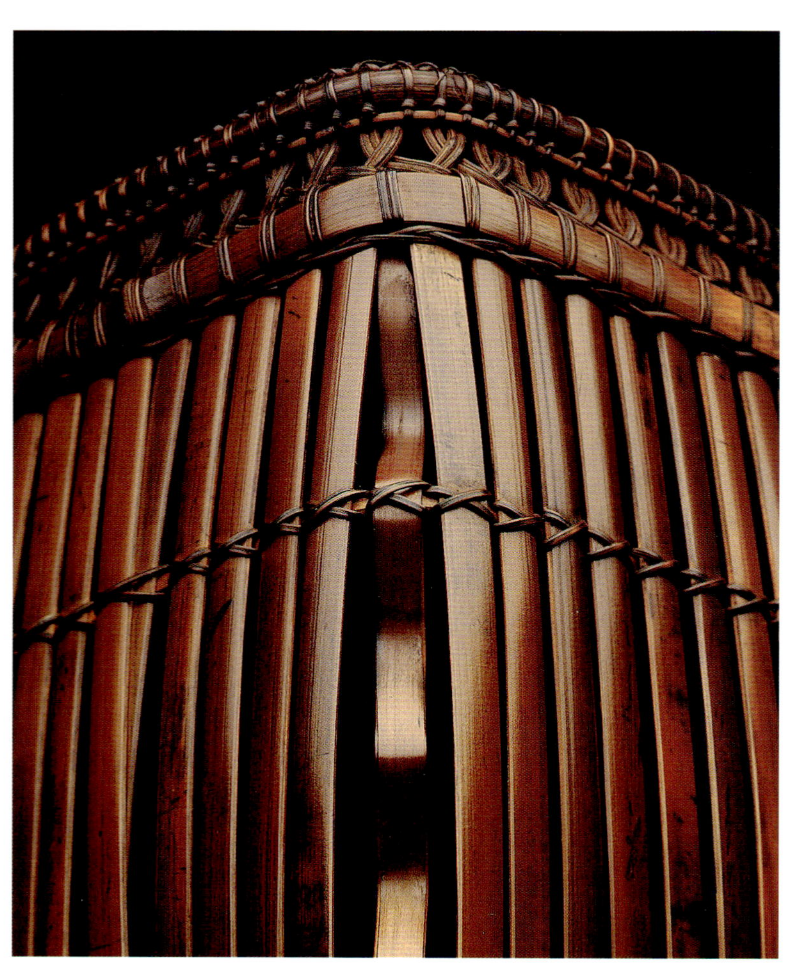

Dawn

1976
5 1/2" x 5 1/2" x 10" (14 x 14 x 25 cm)

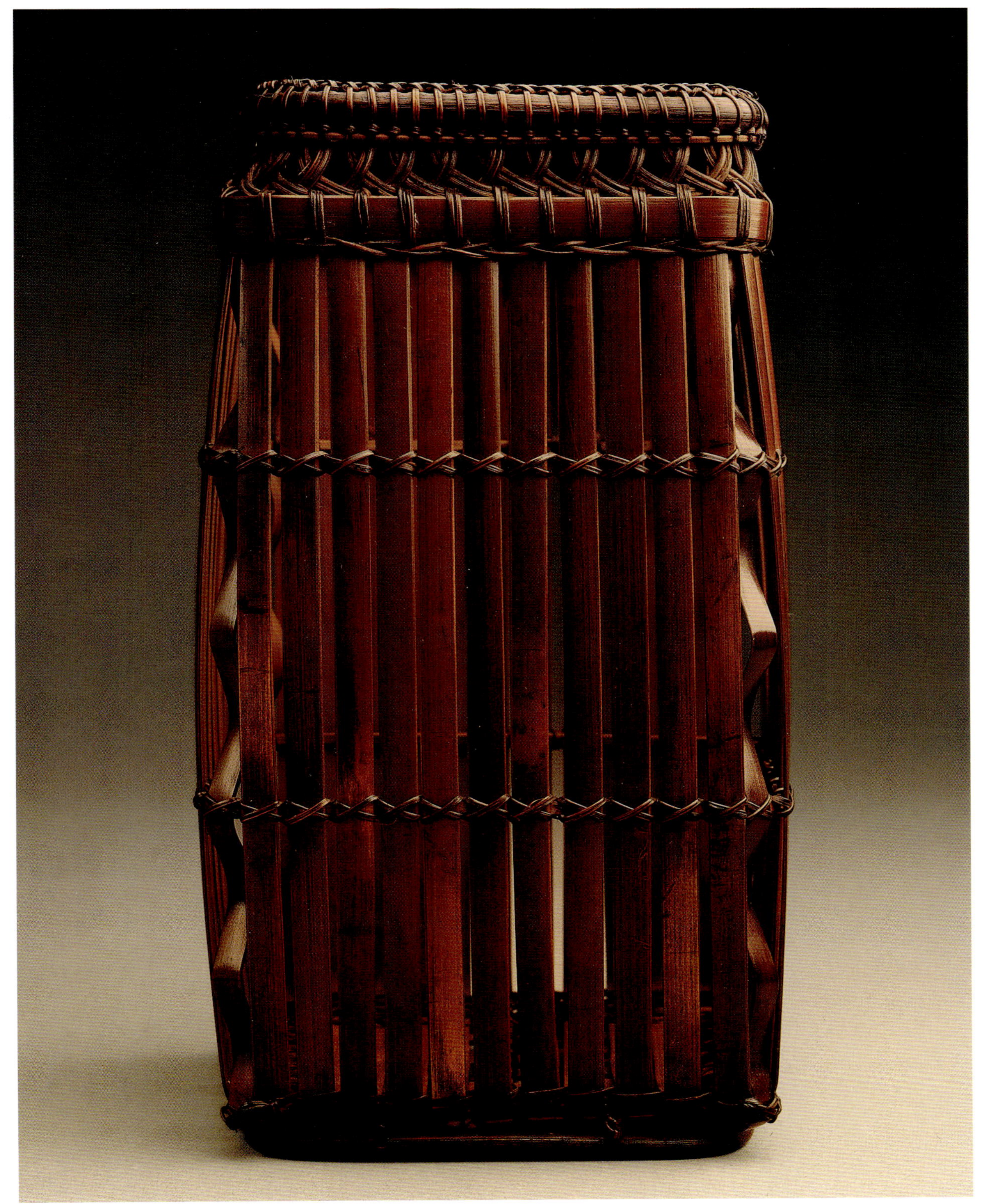

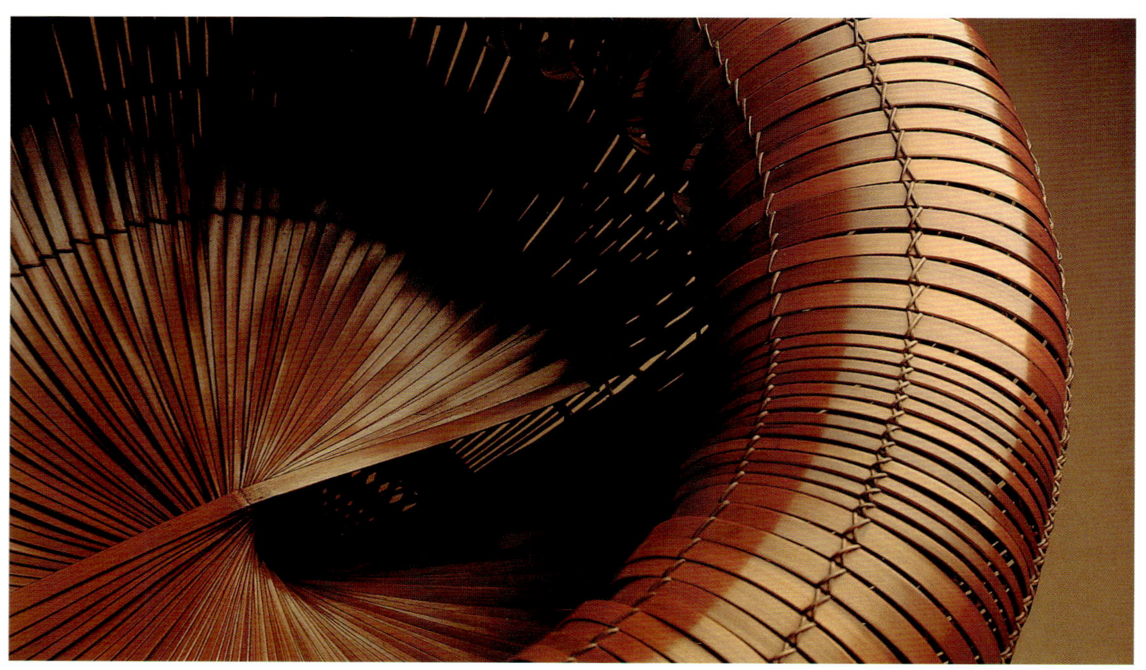

Sound of the Whirlpool

1977
21"d x 10" (53 x 25 cm)

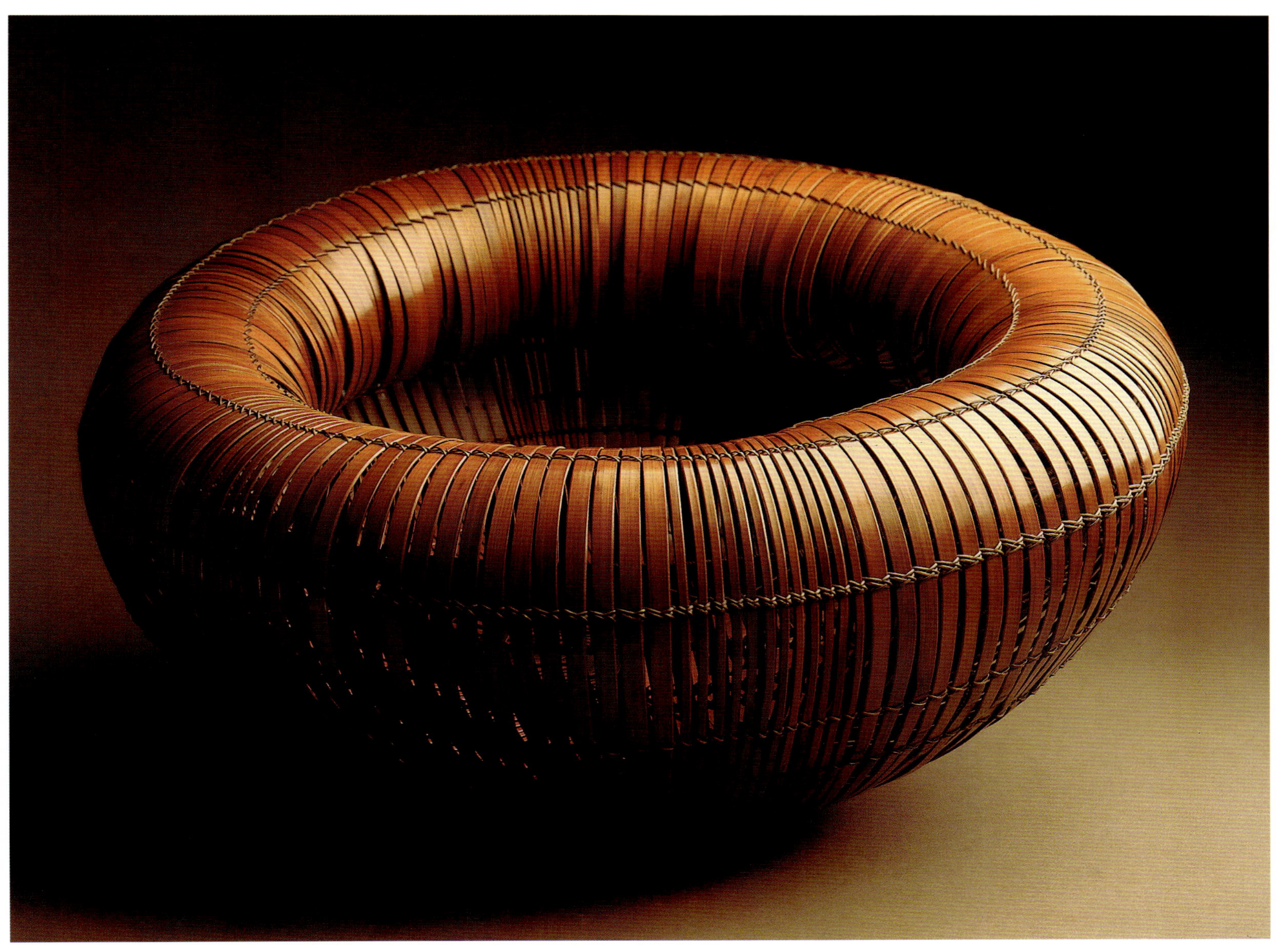

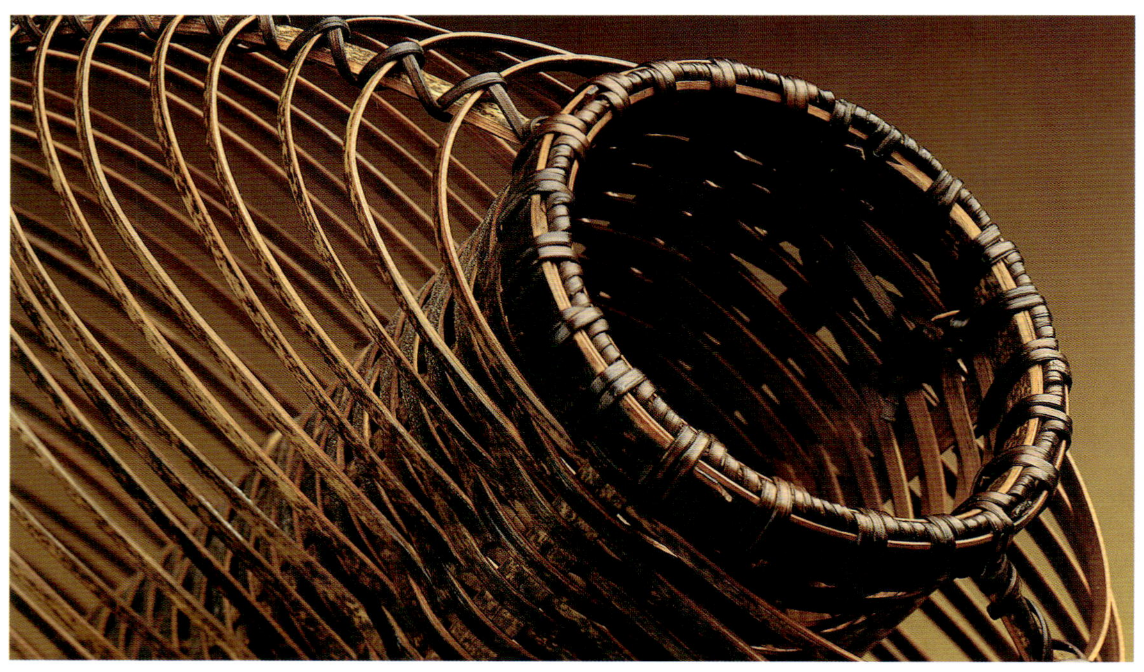

Hazy Appearance

1977
8 2/1" x 3" x 8 1/2" (22 x 8 x 22 cm)

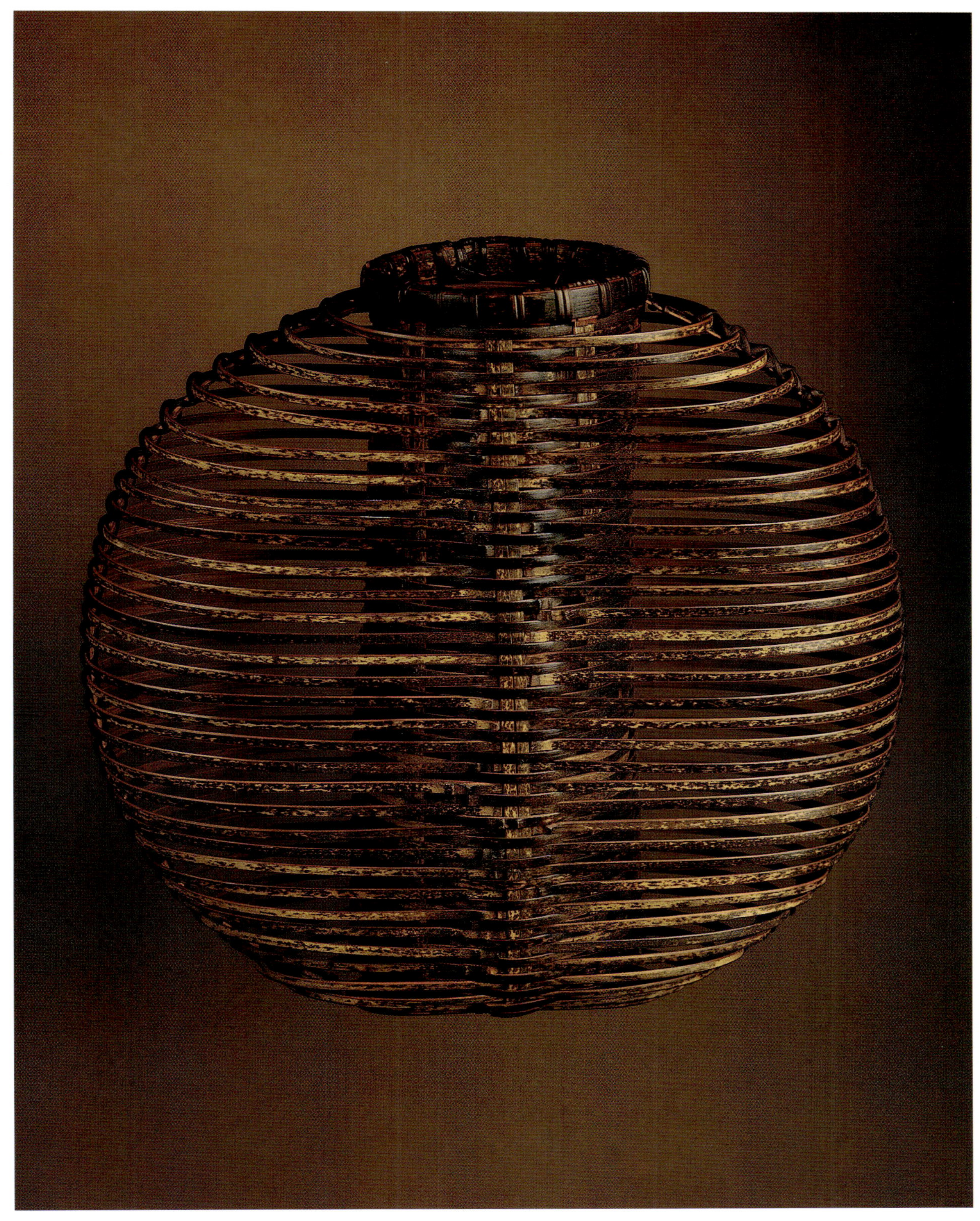

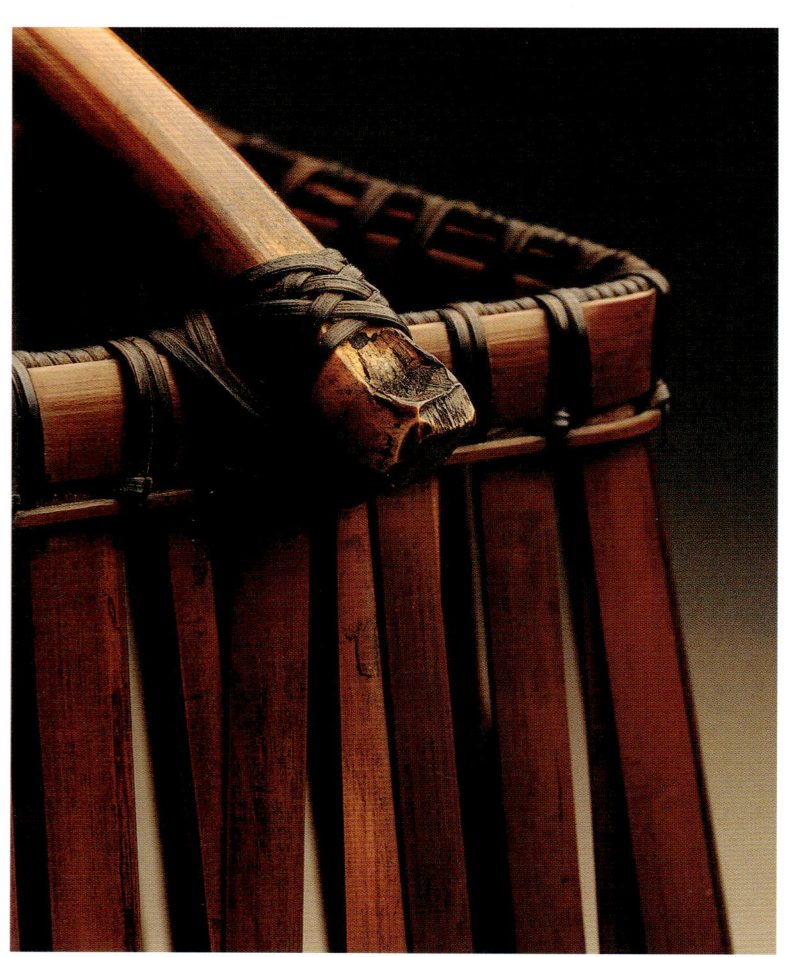

Bamboo Grove

1977
18" x 5" x 7" (46 x 13 x 18 cm)

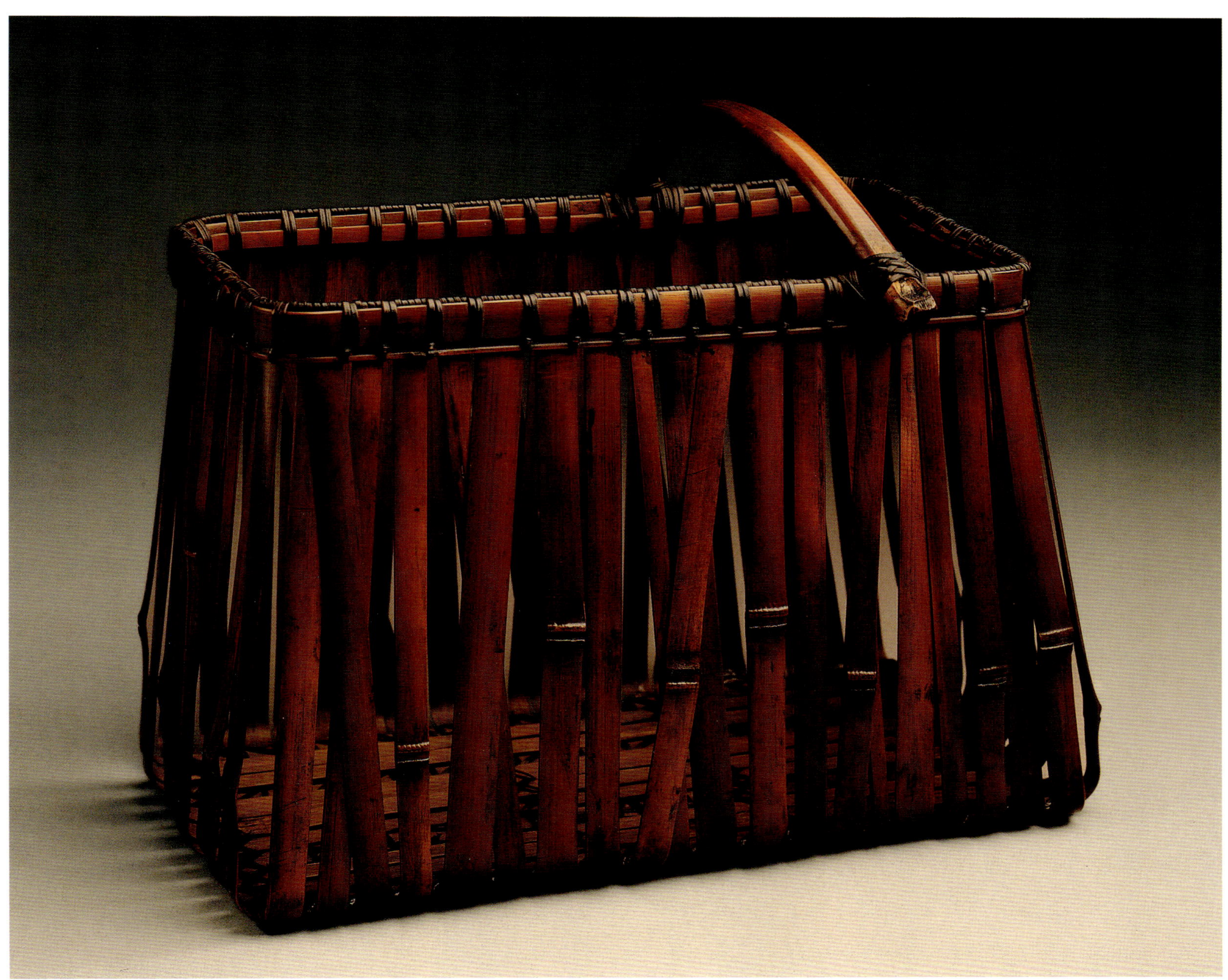

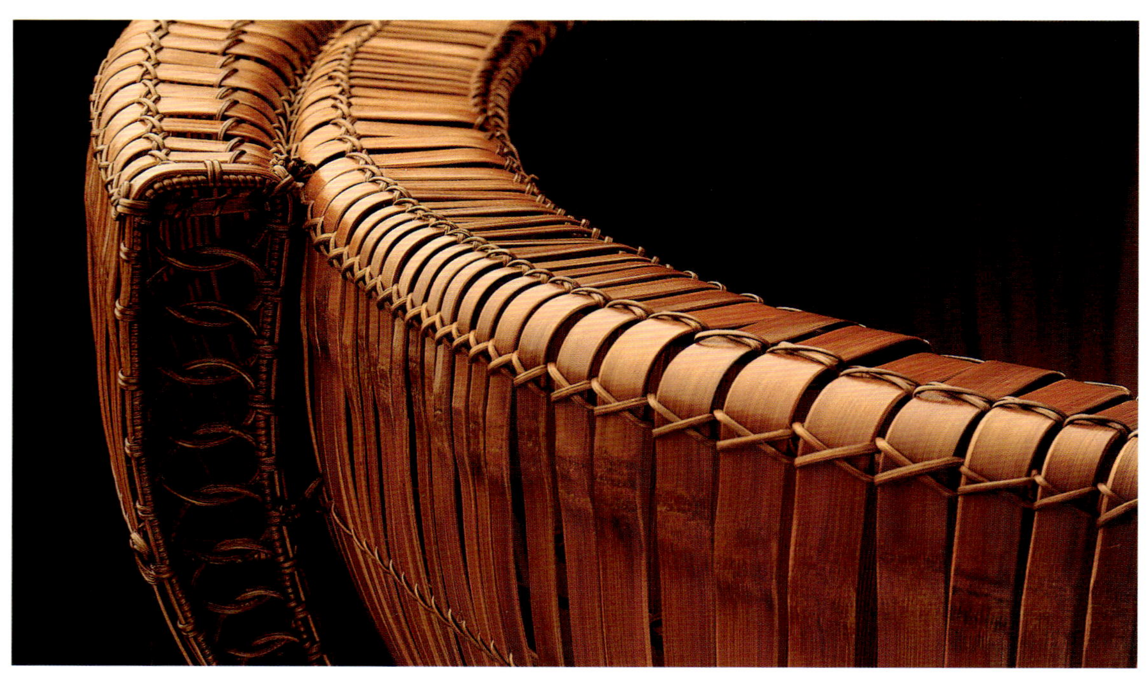

Ocean Whirlpool

1978
24"d x 7" (61 x 18 cm)

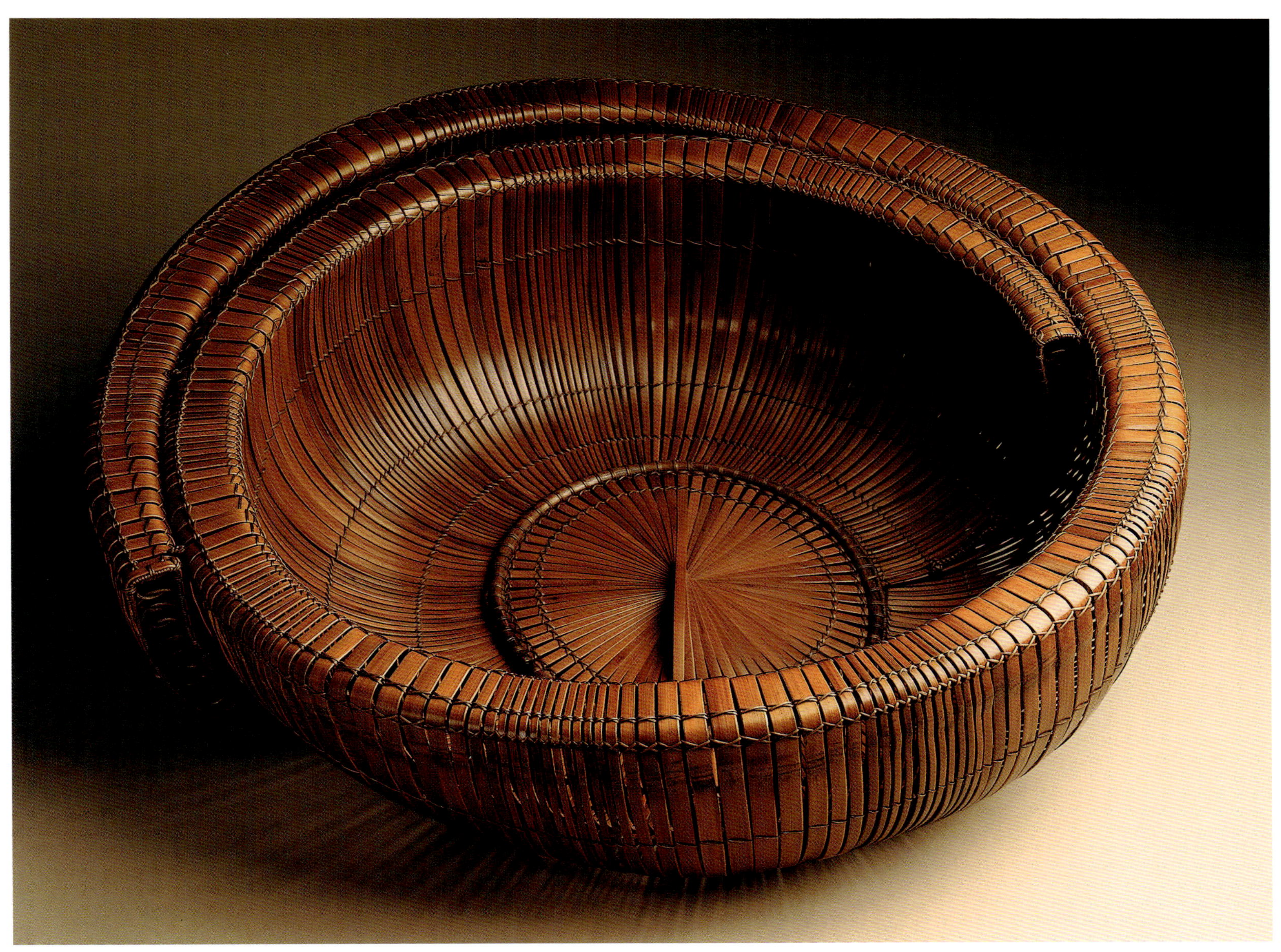

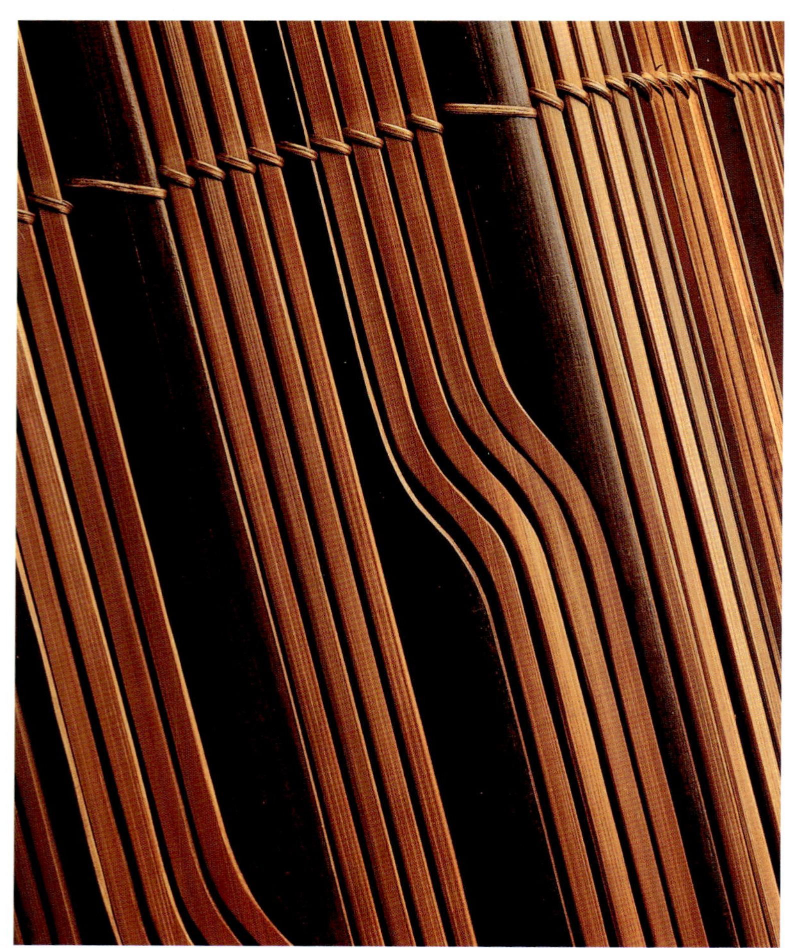

Reflection Through Standing Trees

1978
7 1/2"d x 12" (19 x 30 cm)

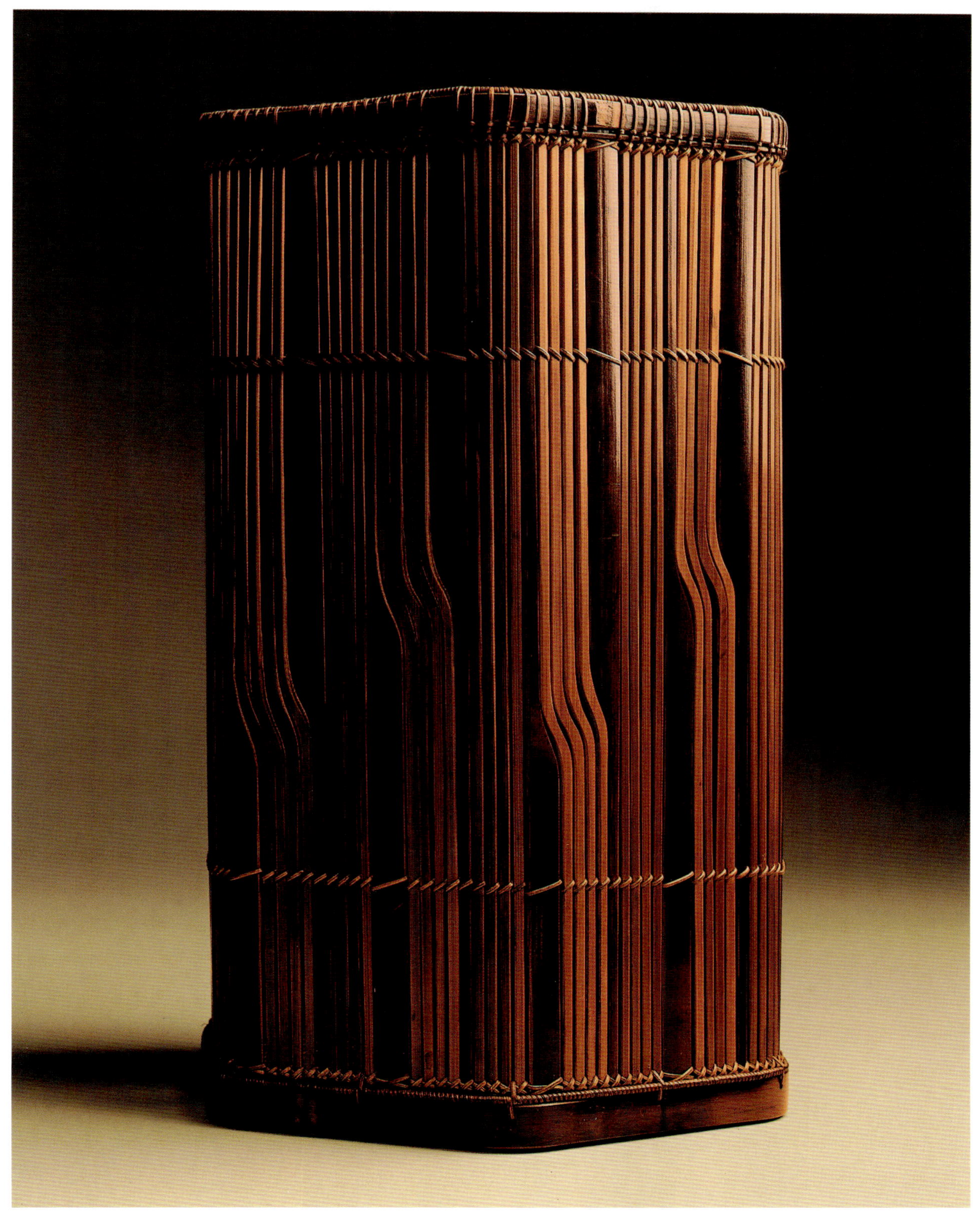

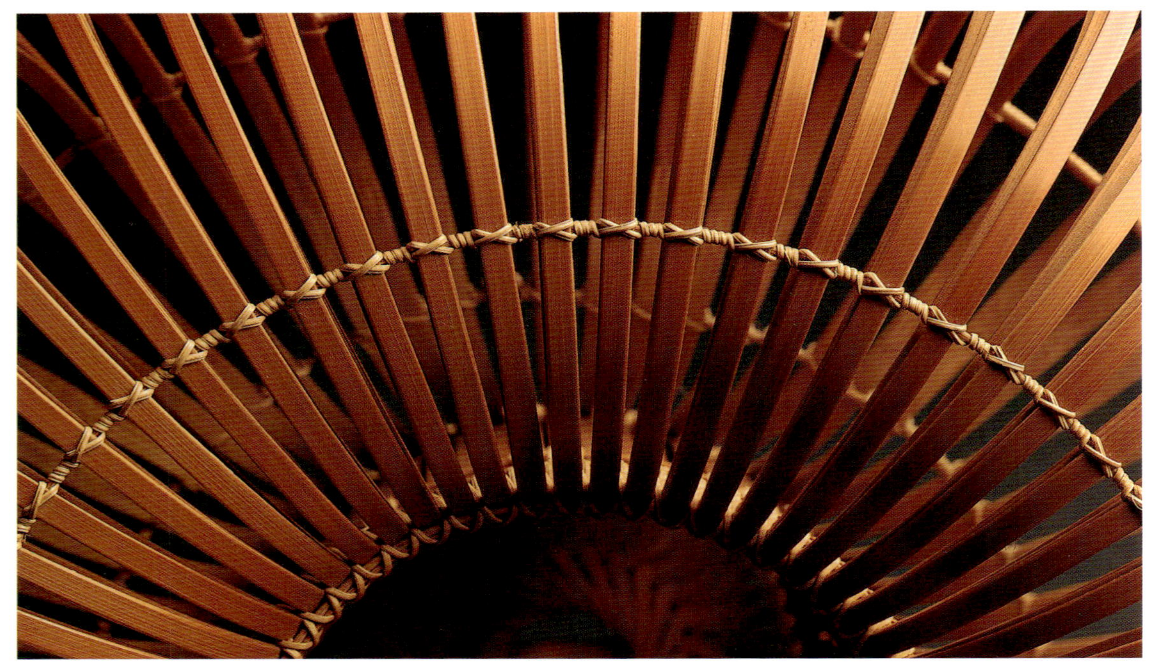

Pure Spring

1978
7 1/2"d x 13 1/2 (19d x 34 cm)

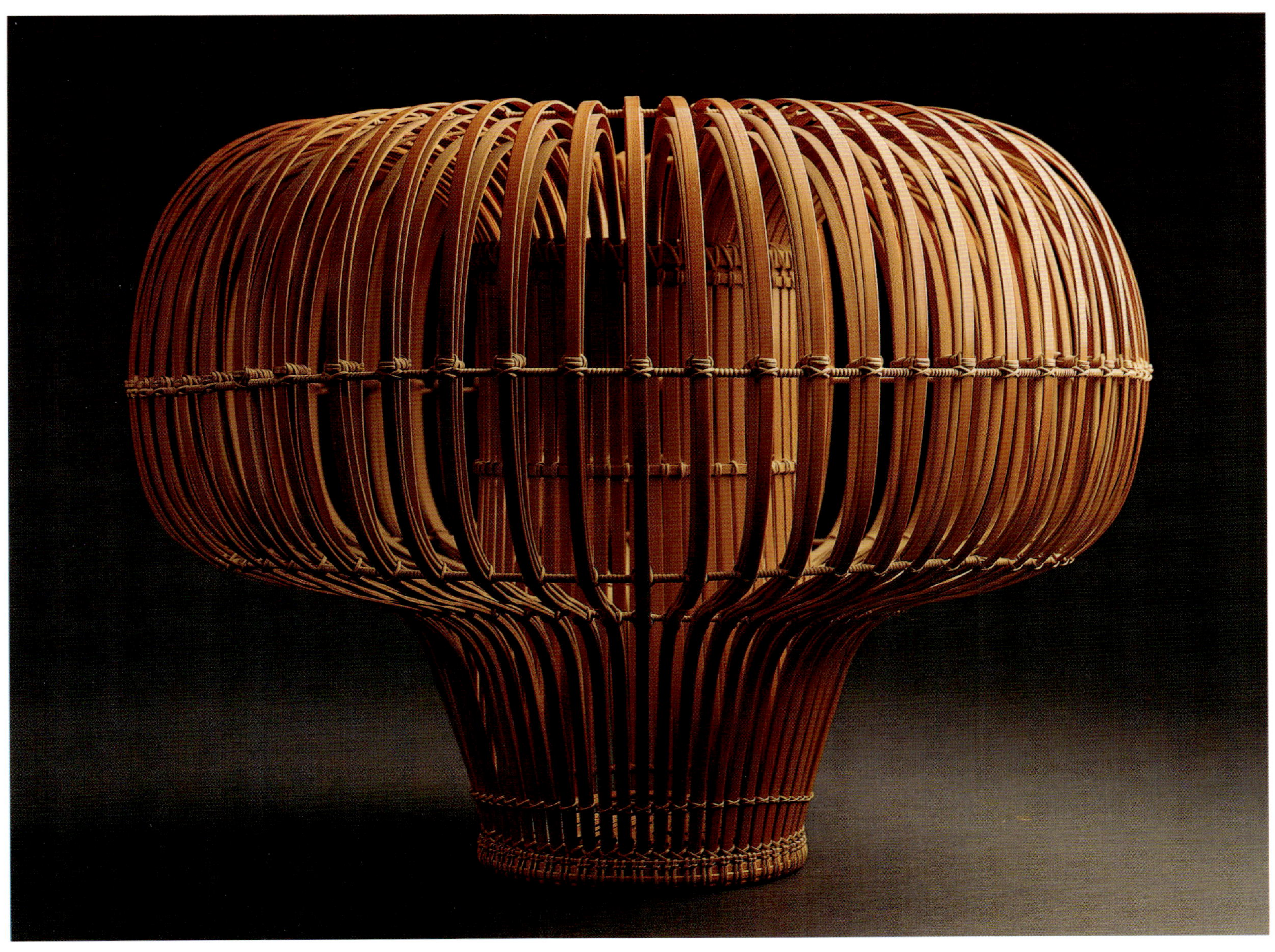

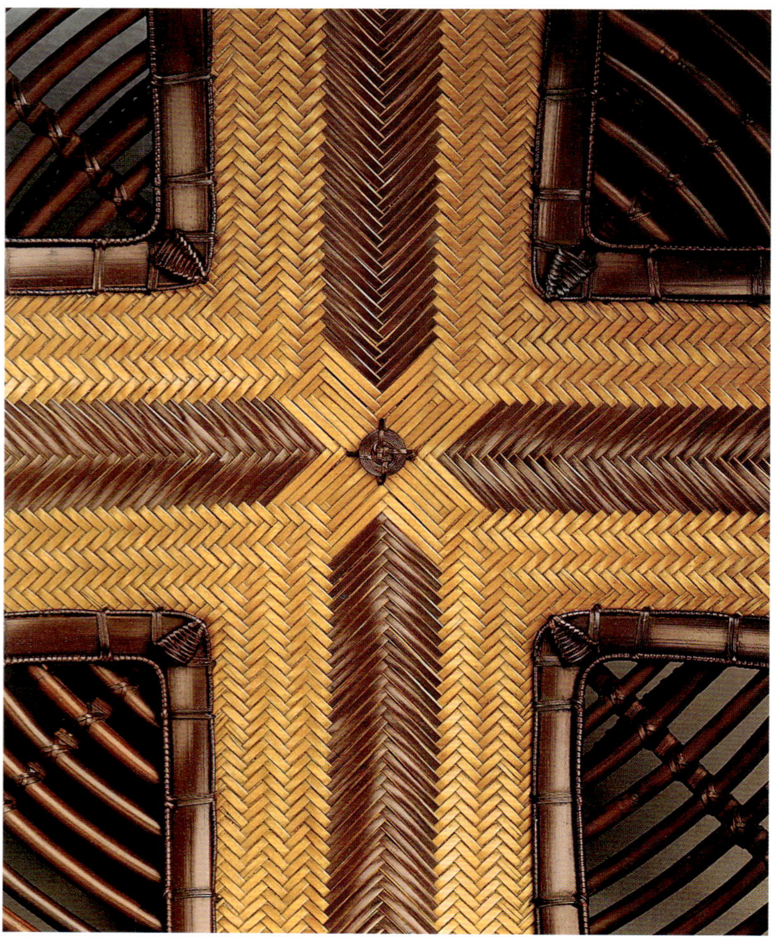

Cross Pattern Basket

1978
19"d x 7" (48 x 18 cm)

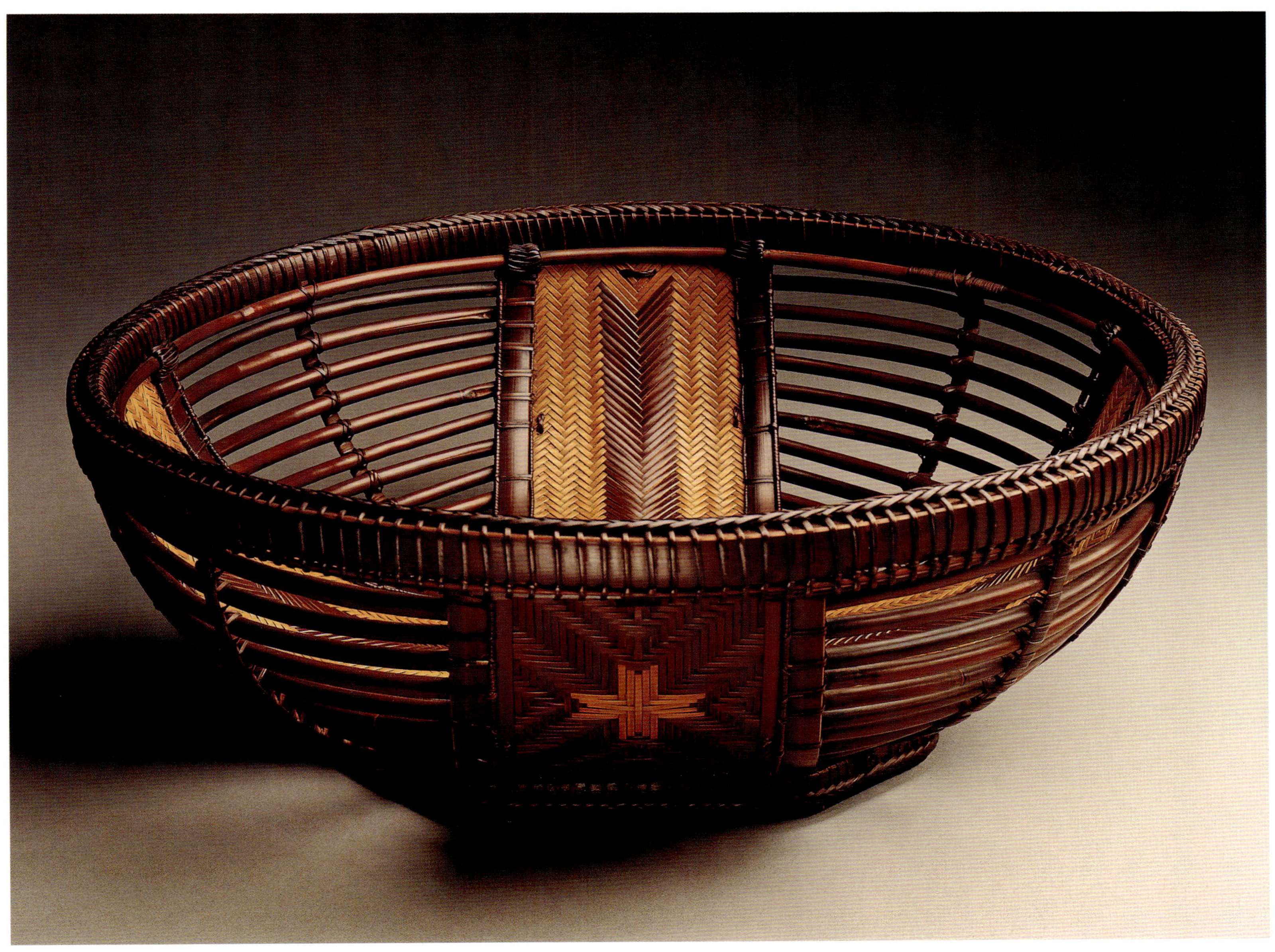

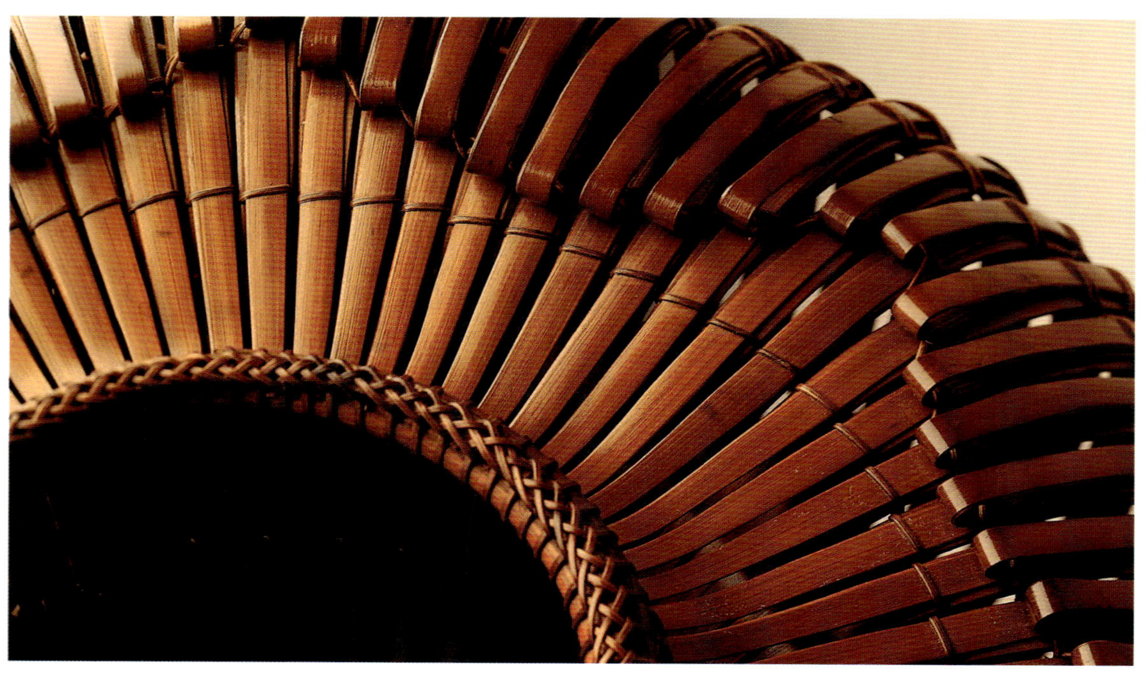

Flower Bud

1980
13"d x 8 1/2" (33 x 22 cm)

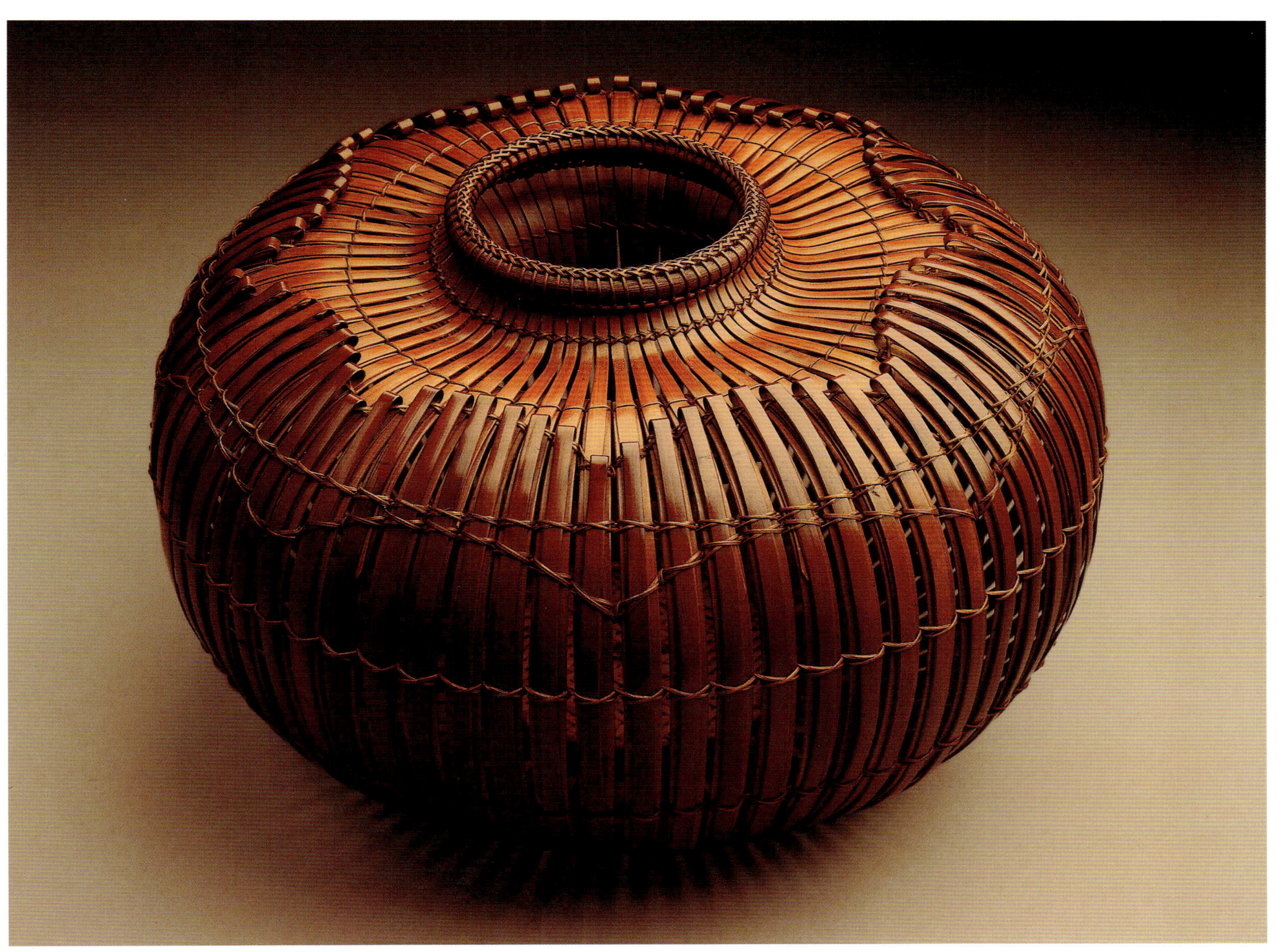

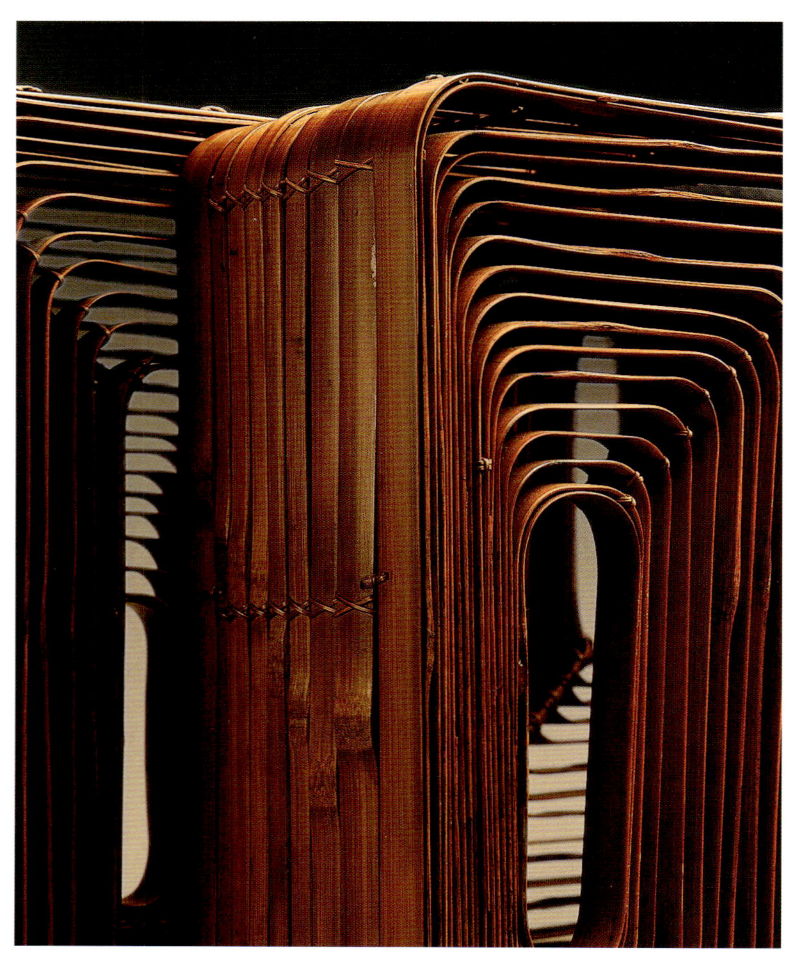

Steep Cliff

1983

24 1/2" x 10" x 8" (62 x 25 x 20 cm)

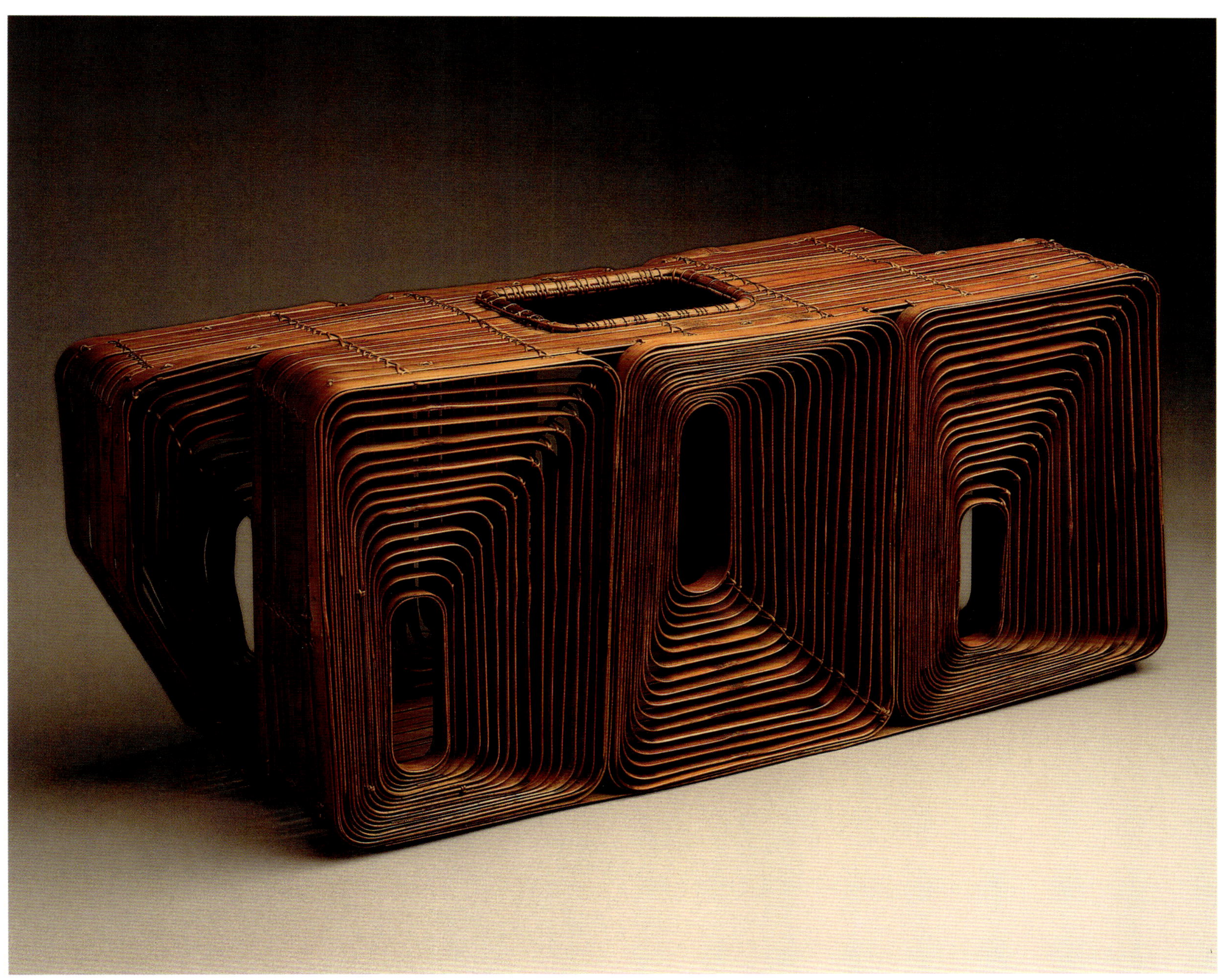

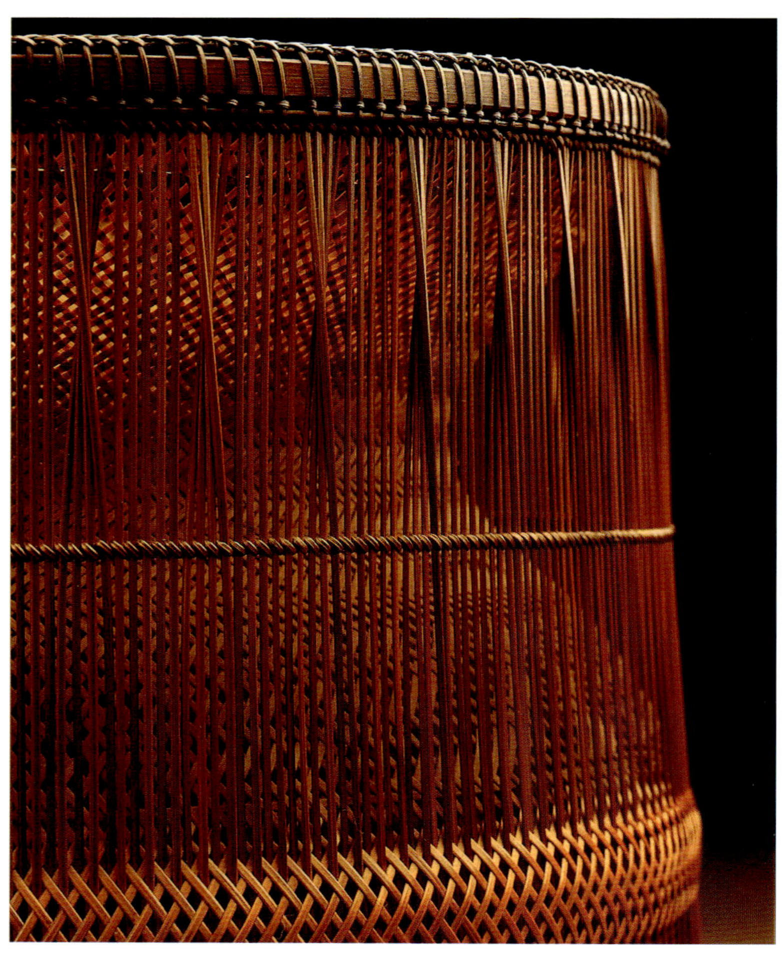

Morning Fog

1983
11"d x 9 1/2" (28 x 24 cm)

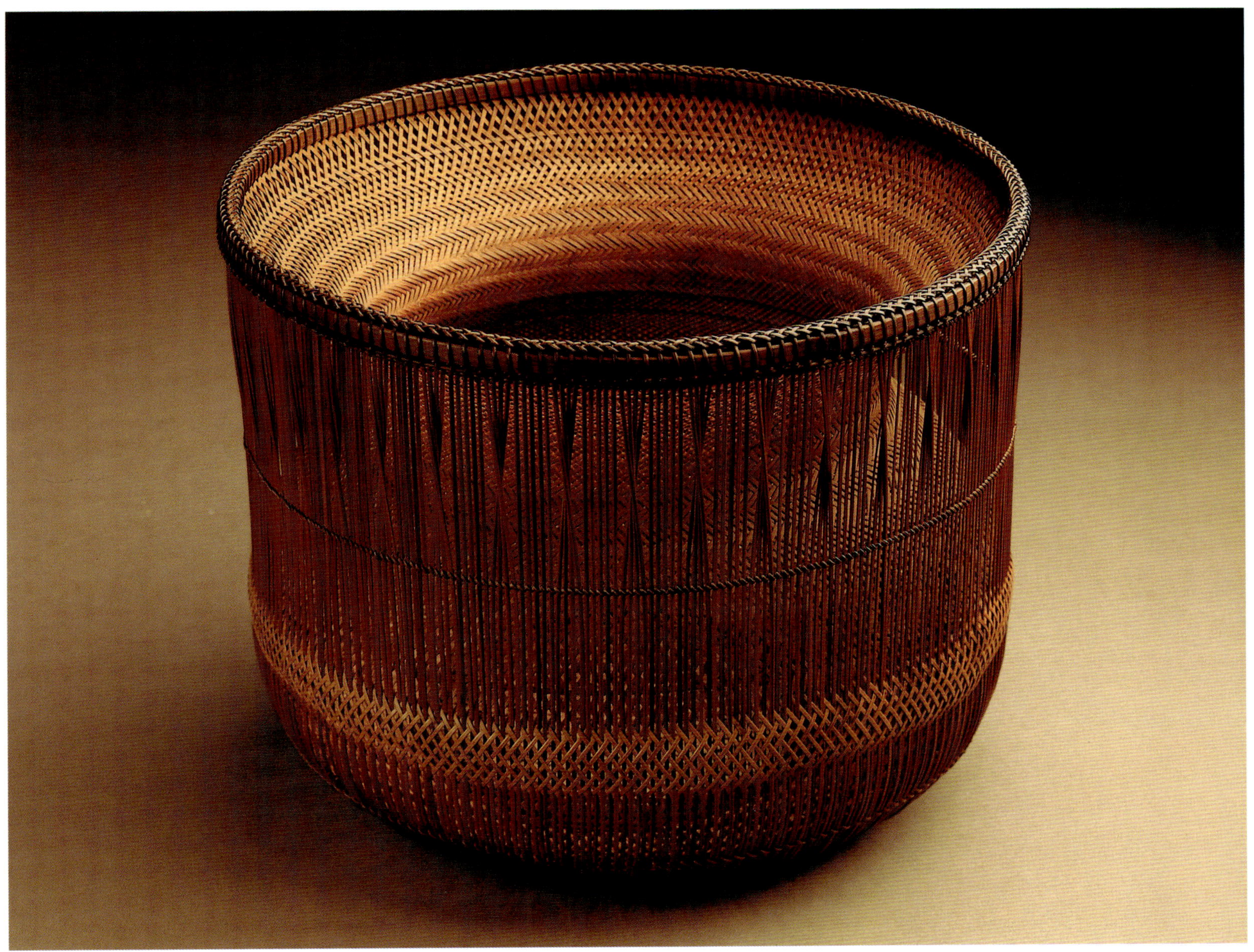

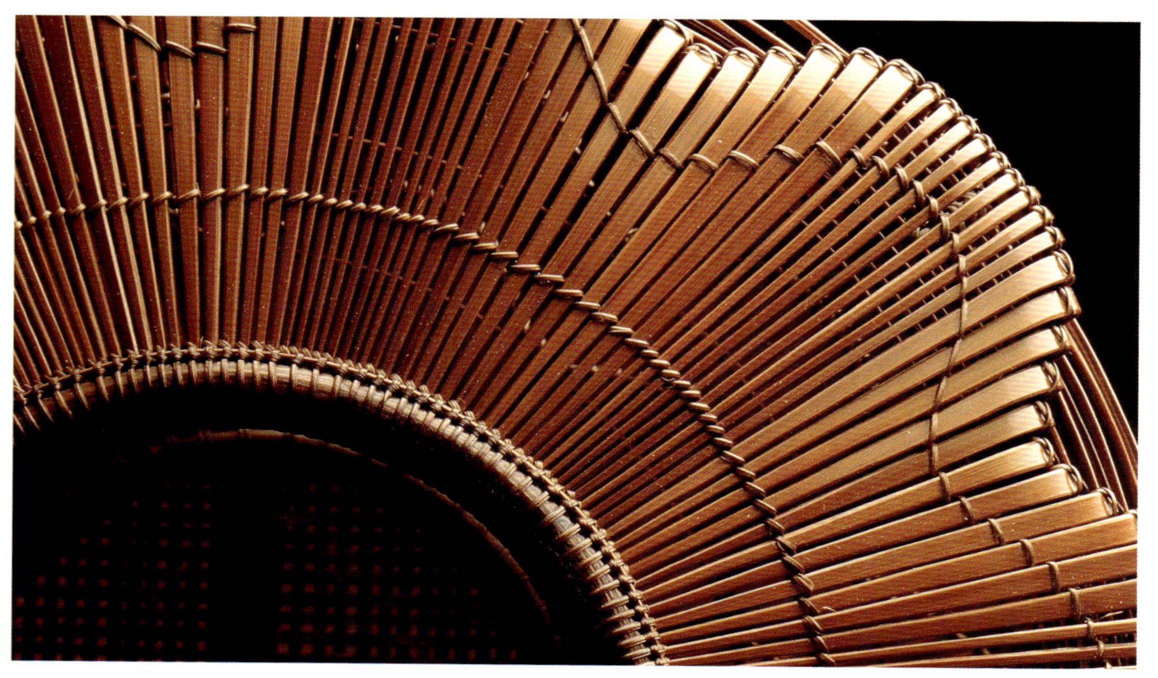

Layered Pattern Flower Basket

1983
15"d x 10" (38 x 25 cm)

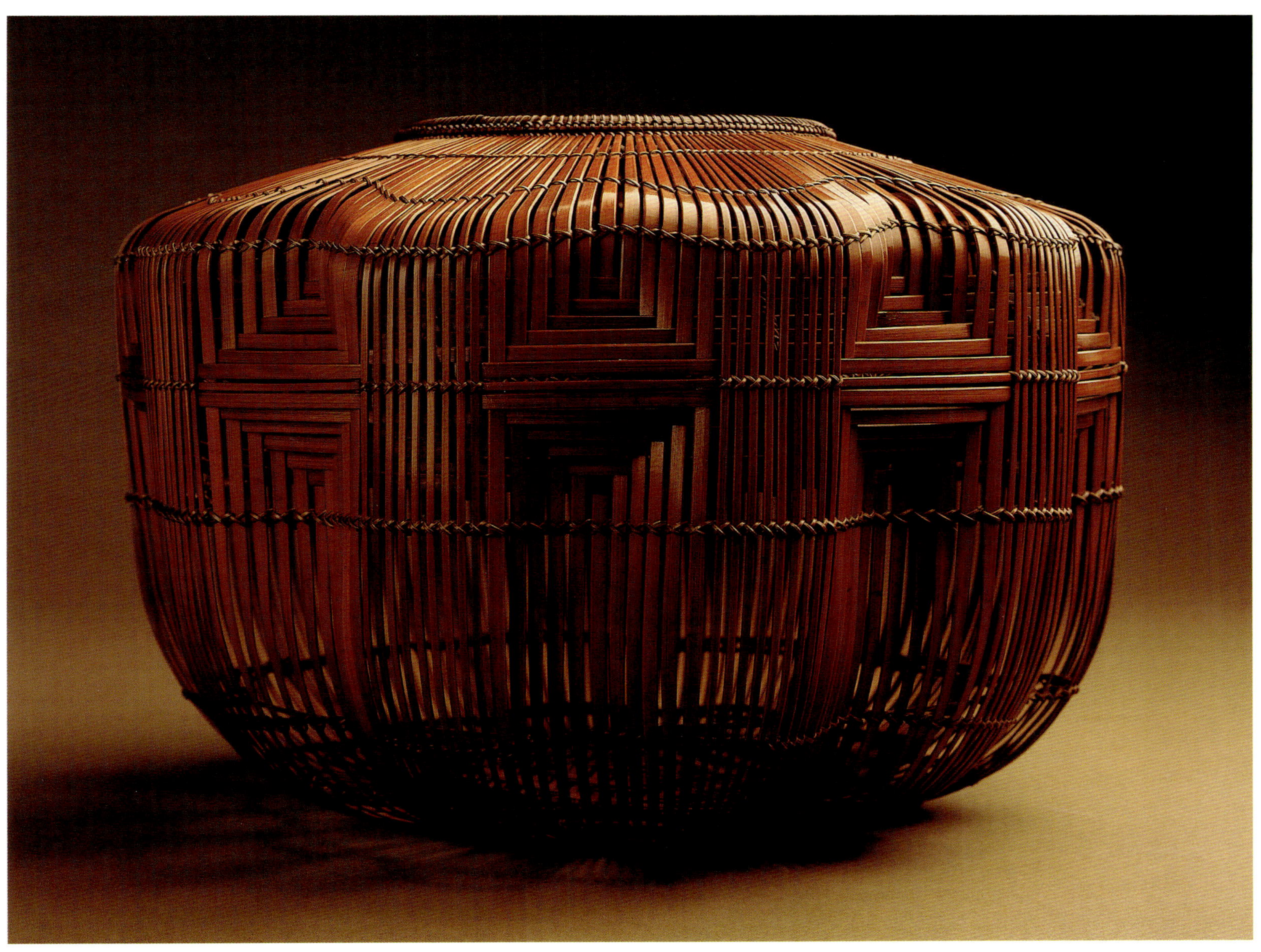

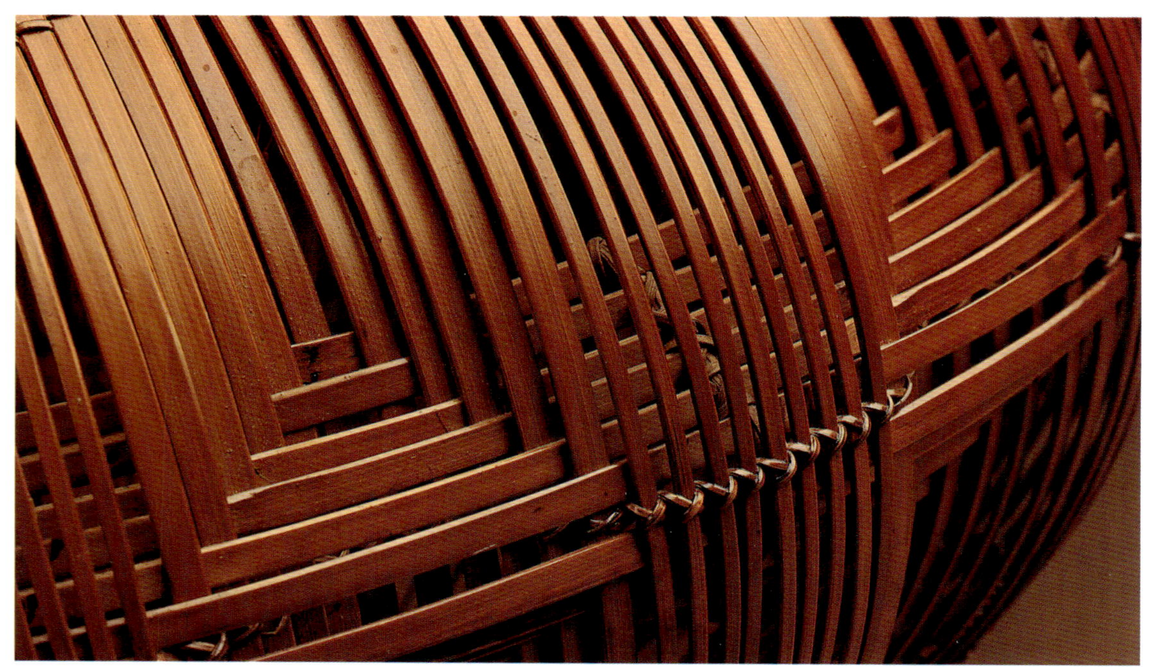

Untitled

1984
15"d x 8" (38 x 20 cm)

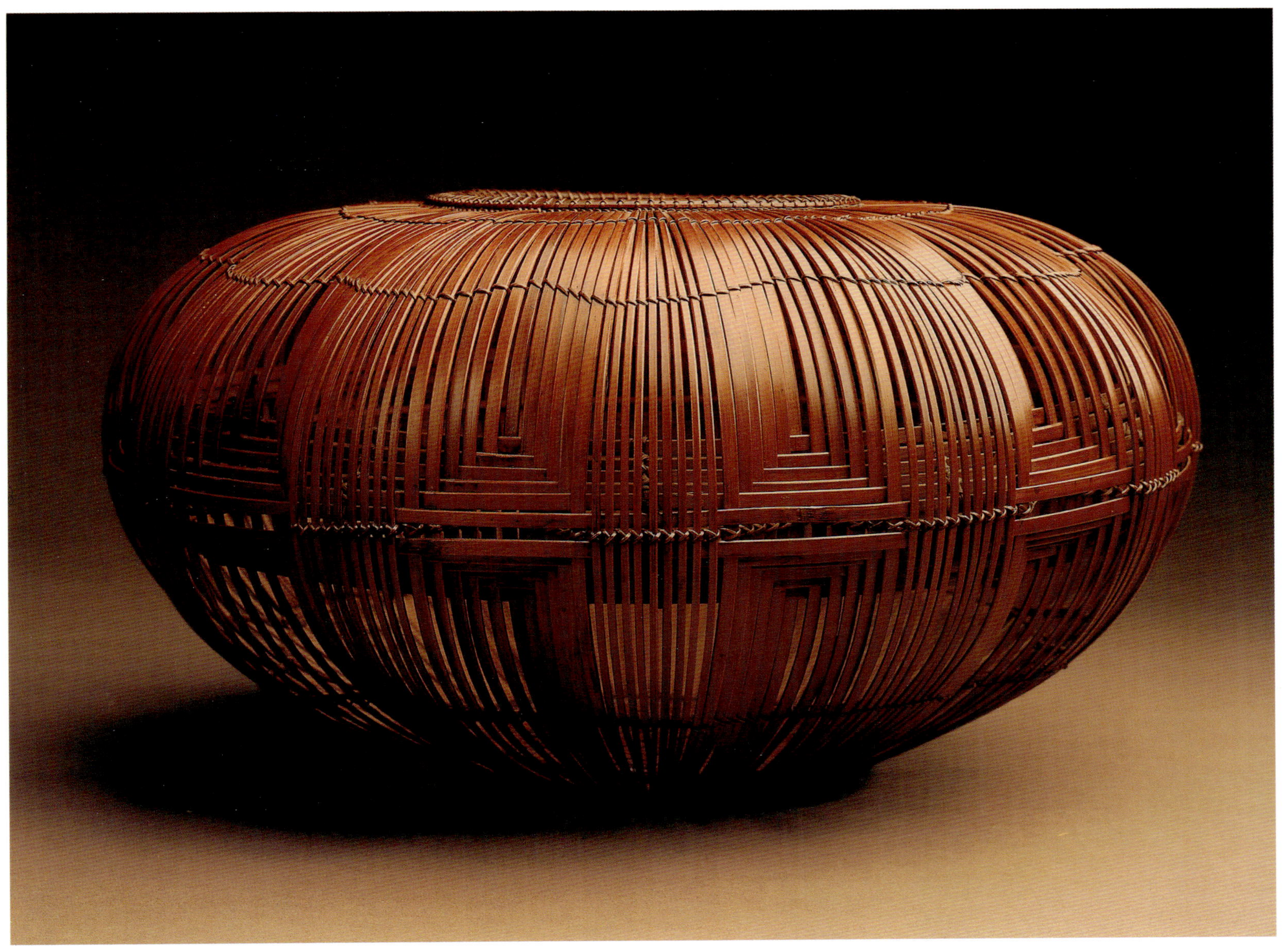

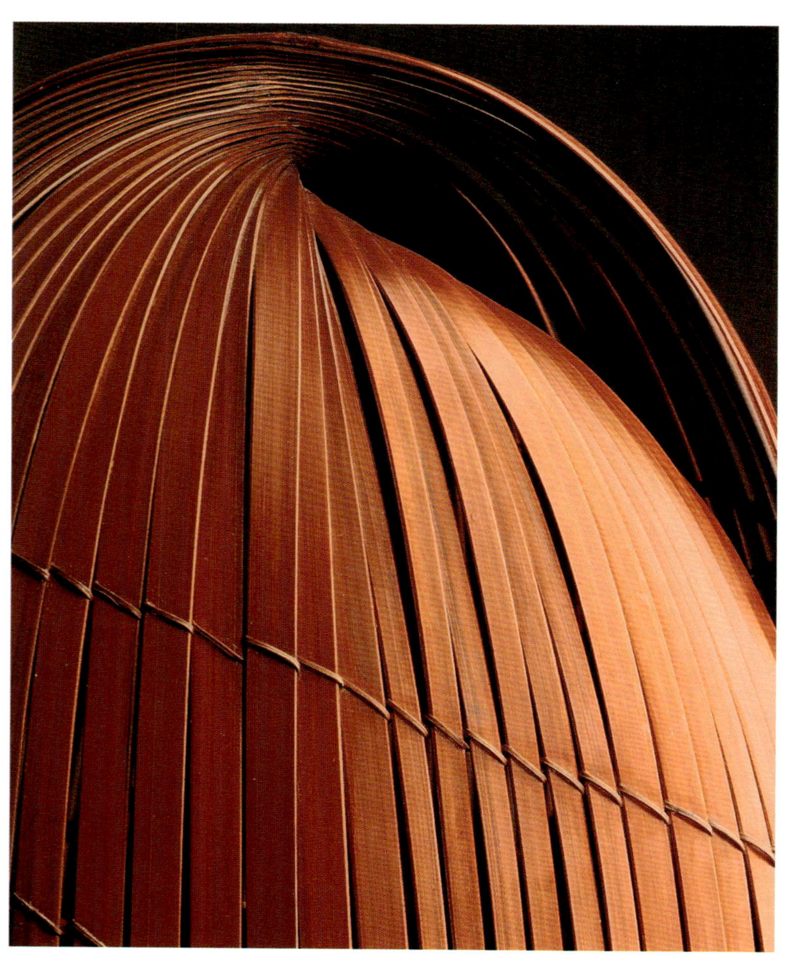

Window

1984
11" x 10" x 23 1/2 " (28 x 26 x 60 cm)

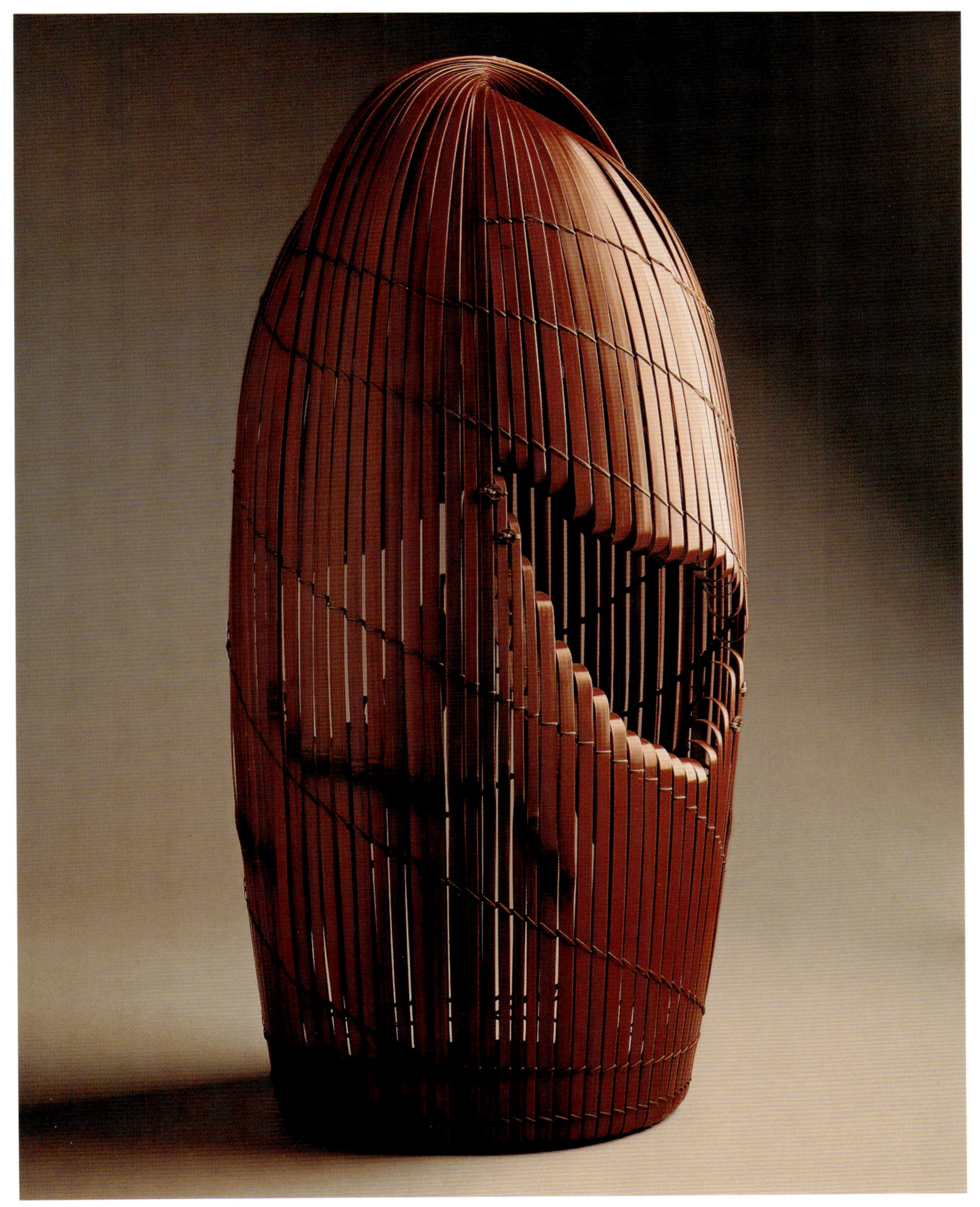

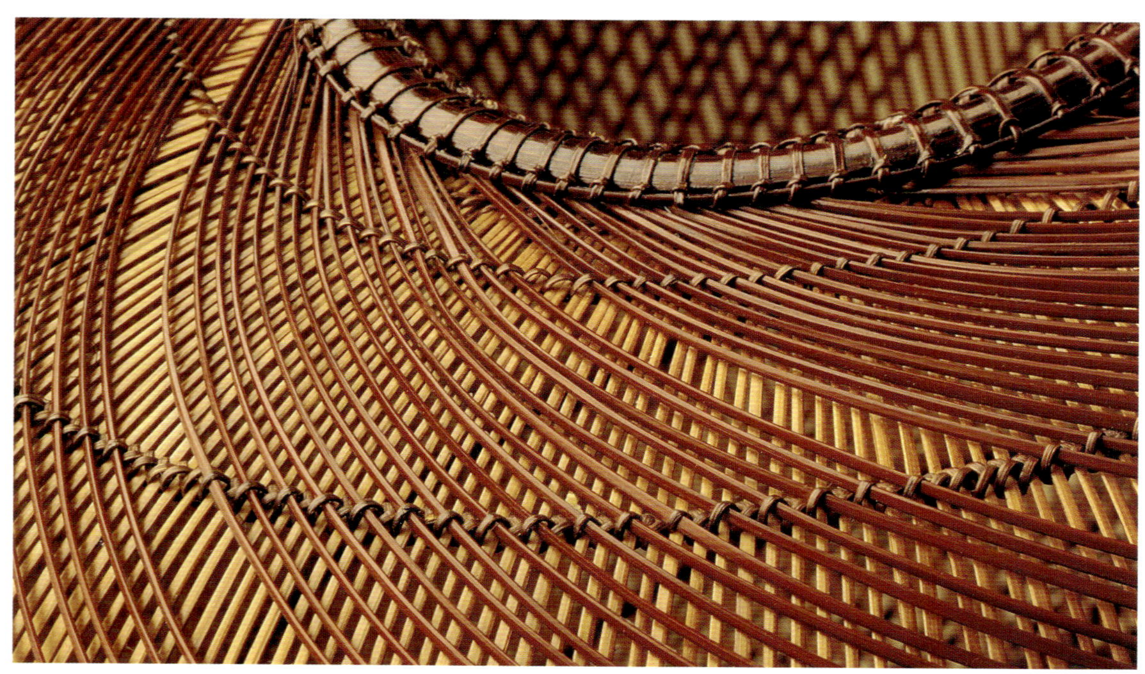

Untitled

1985
19"d x 9" (48d x 23 cm)

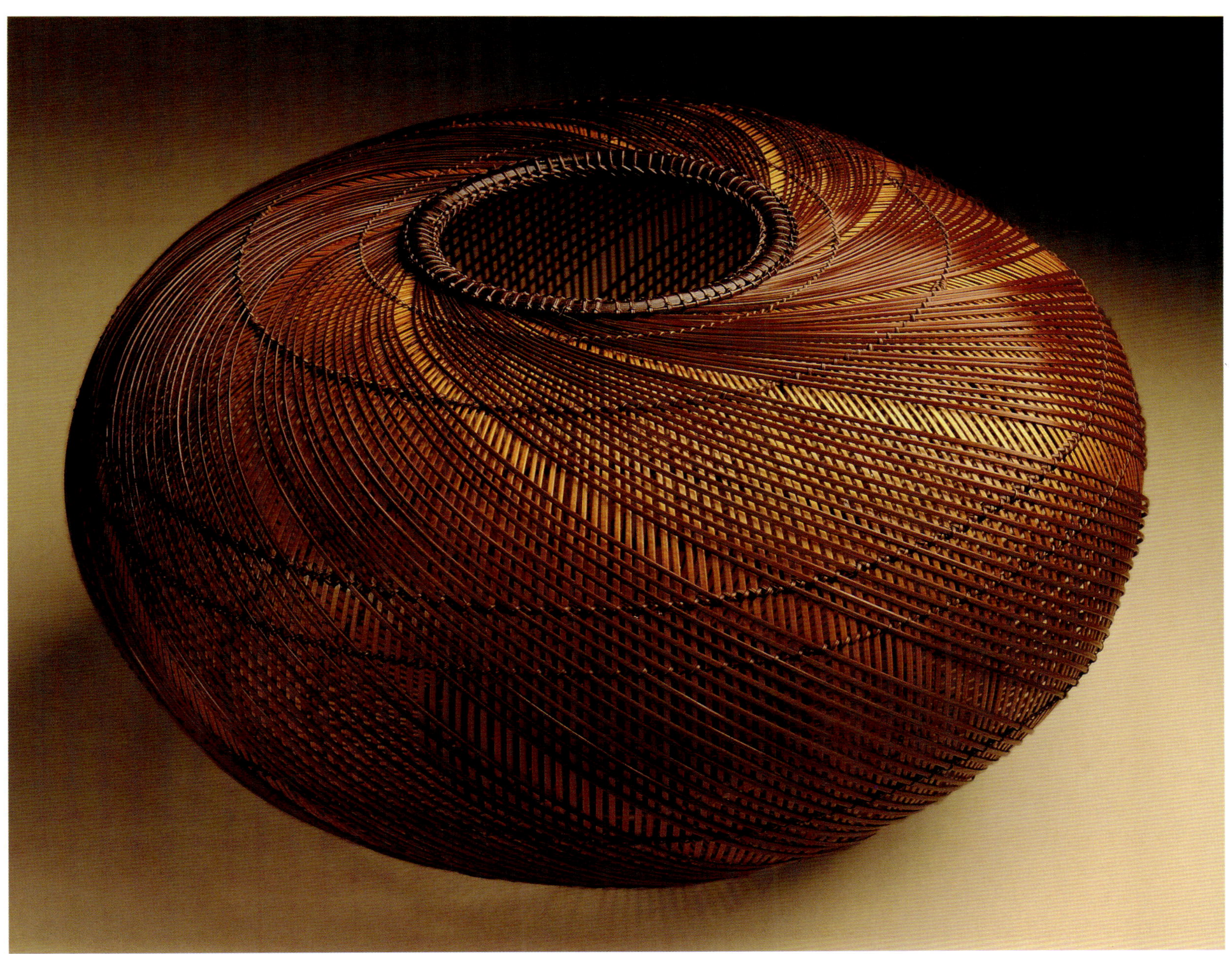

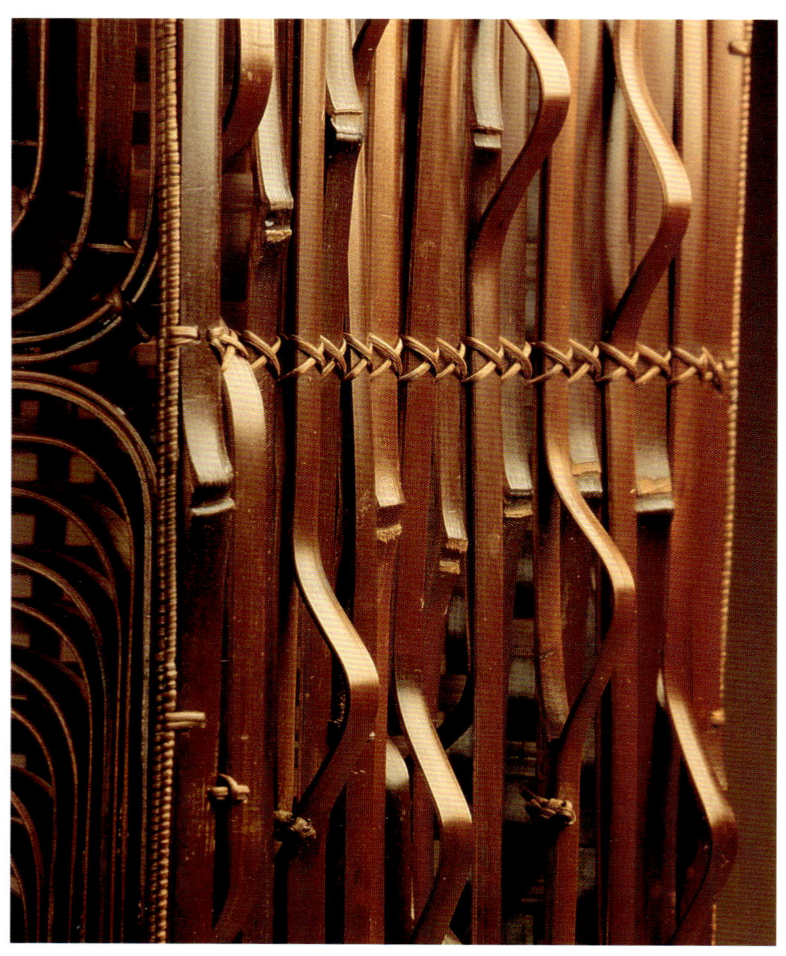

Cliff

1986
15" x 6 1/2" x 7 1/2" (38 x 17 x 19 cm)

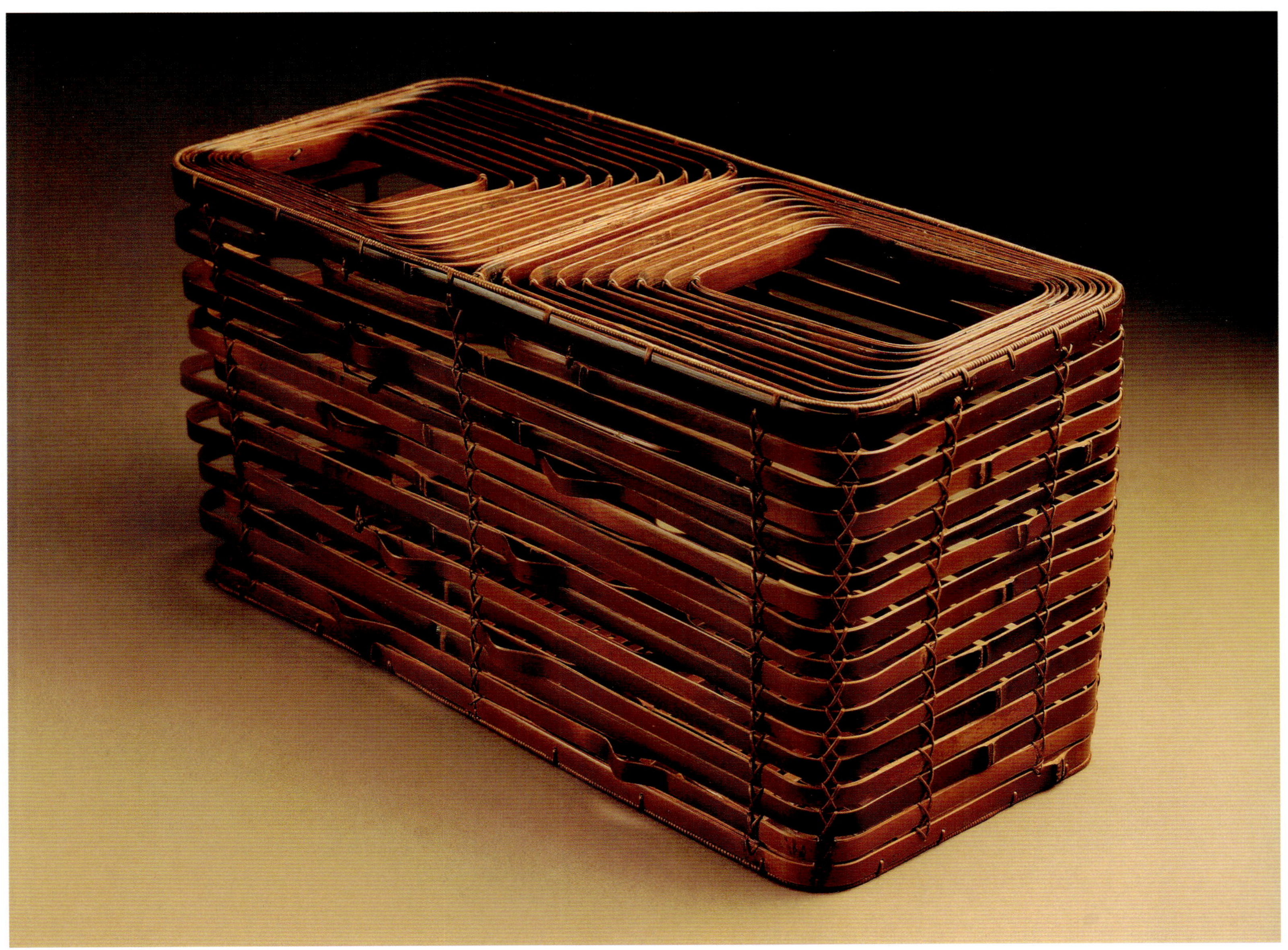

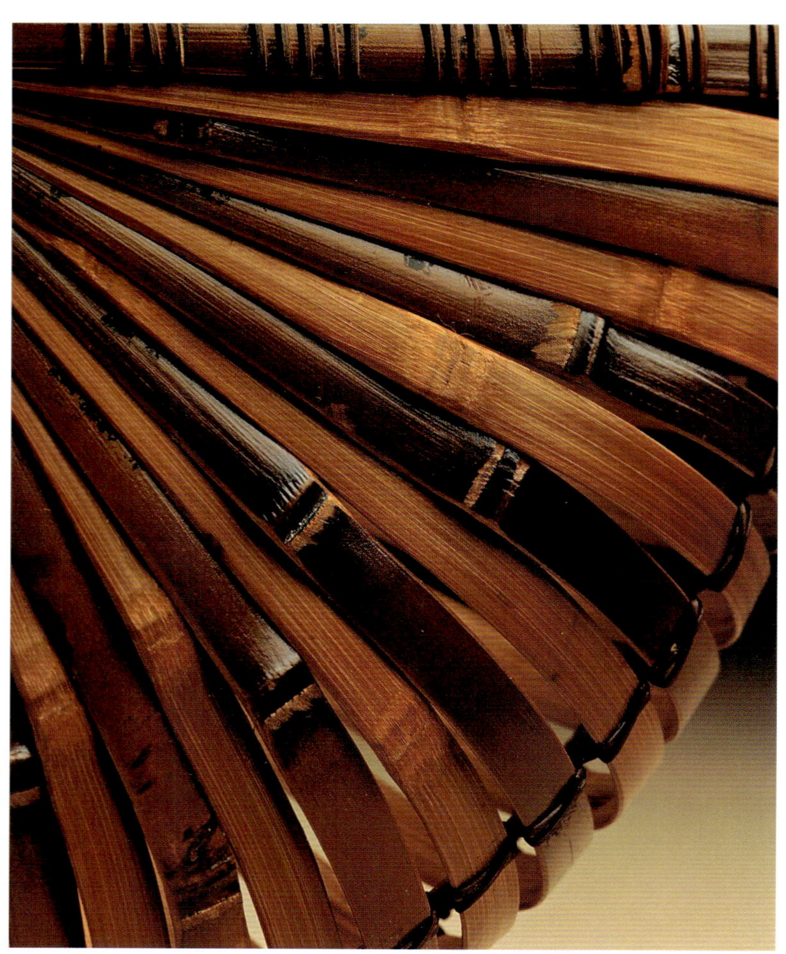

Japanese Fan

1987
14 1/2" x 5" x 7 1/2" (37 x 13 x 19 cm)

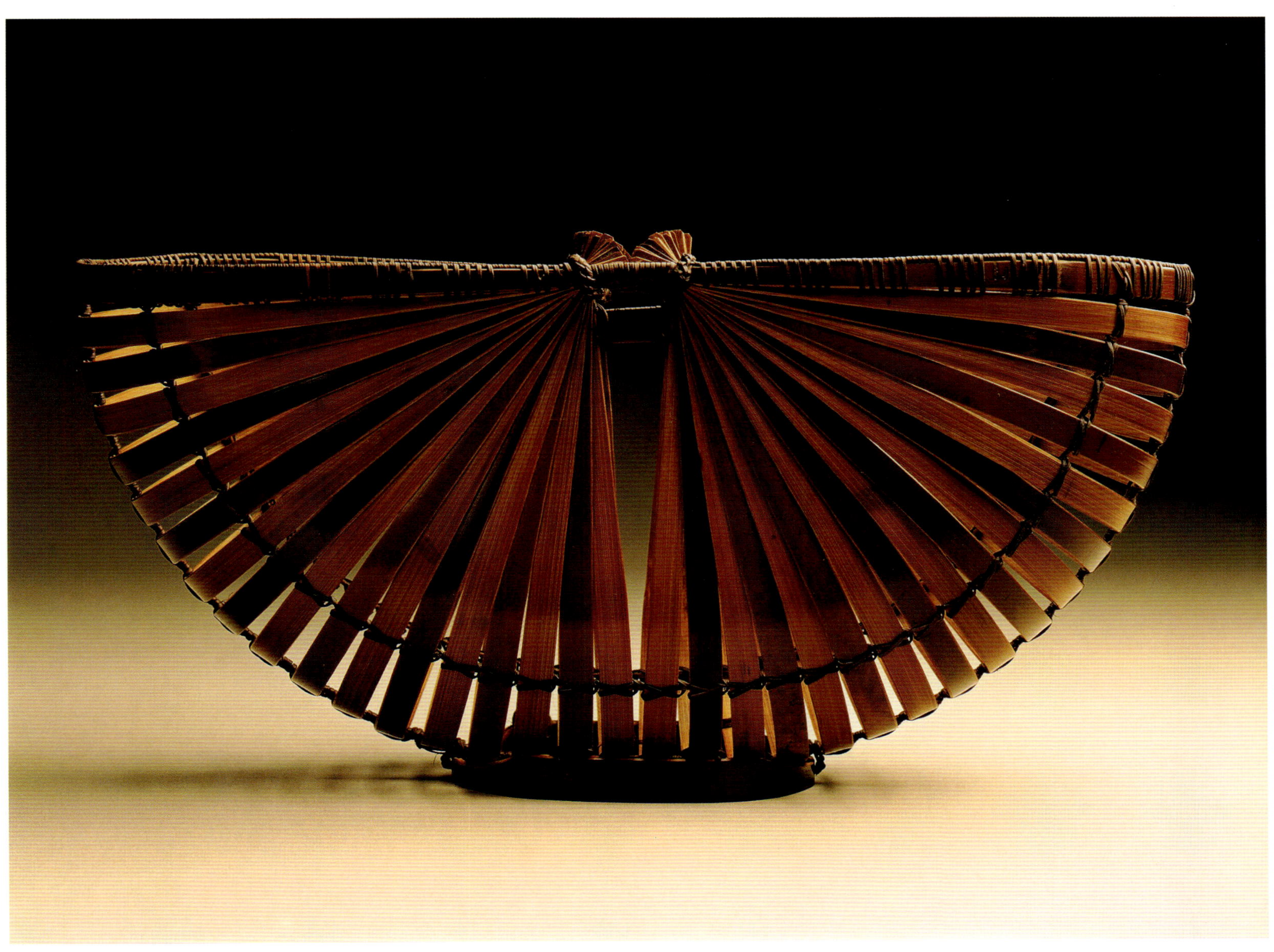

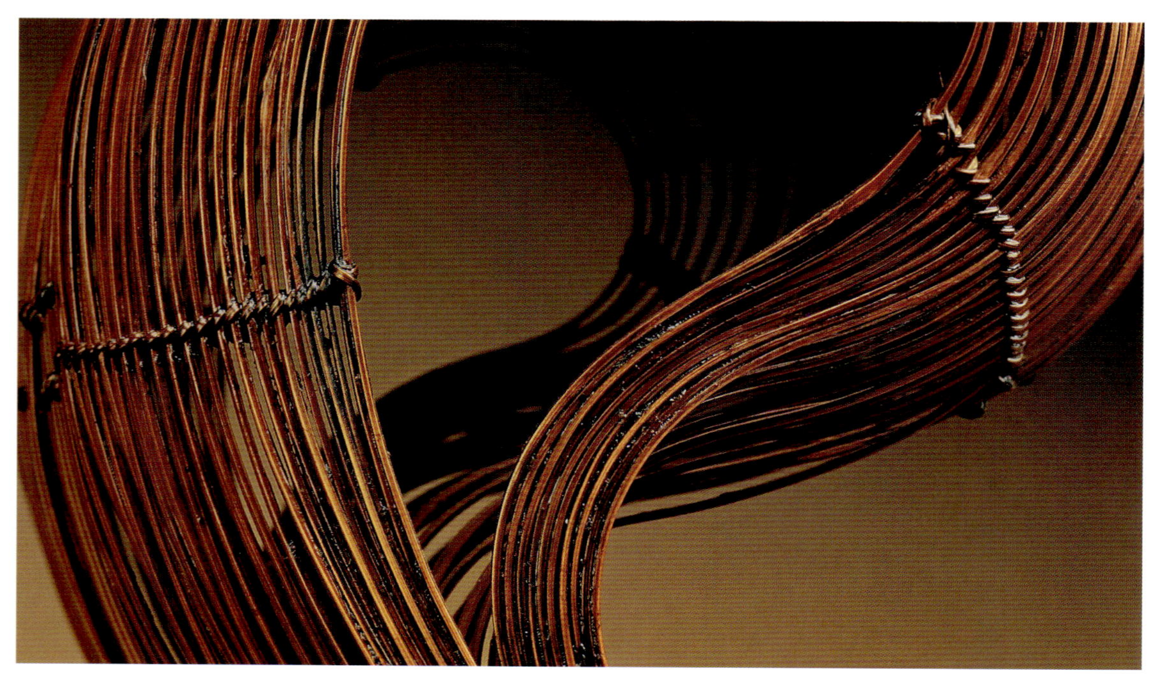

Night Wave

1987
25" x 10" x 10" (64 x 25 x 25 cm)

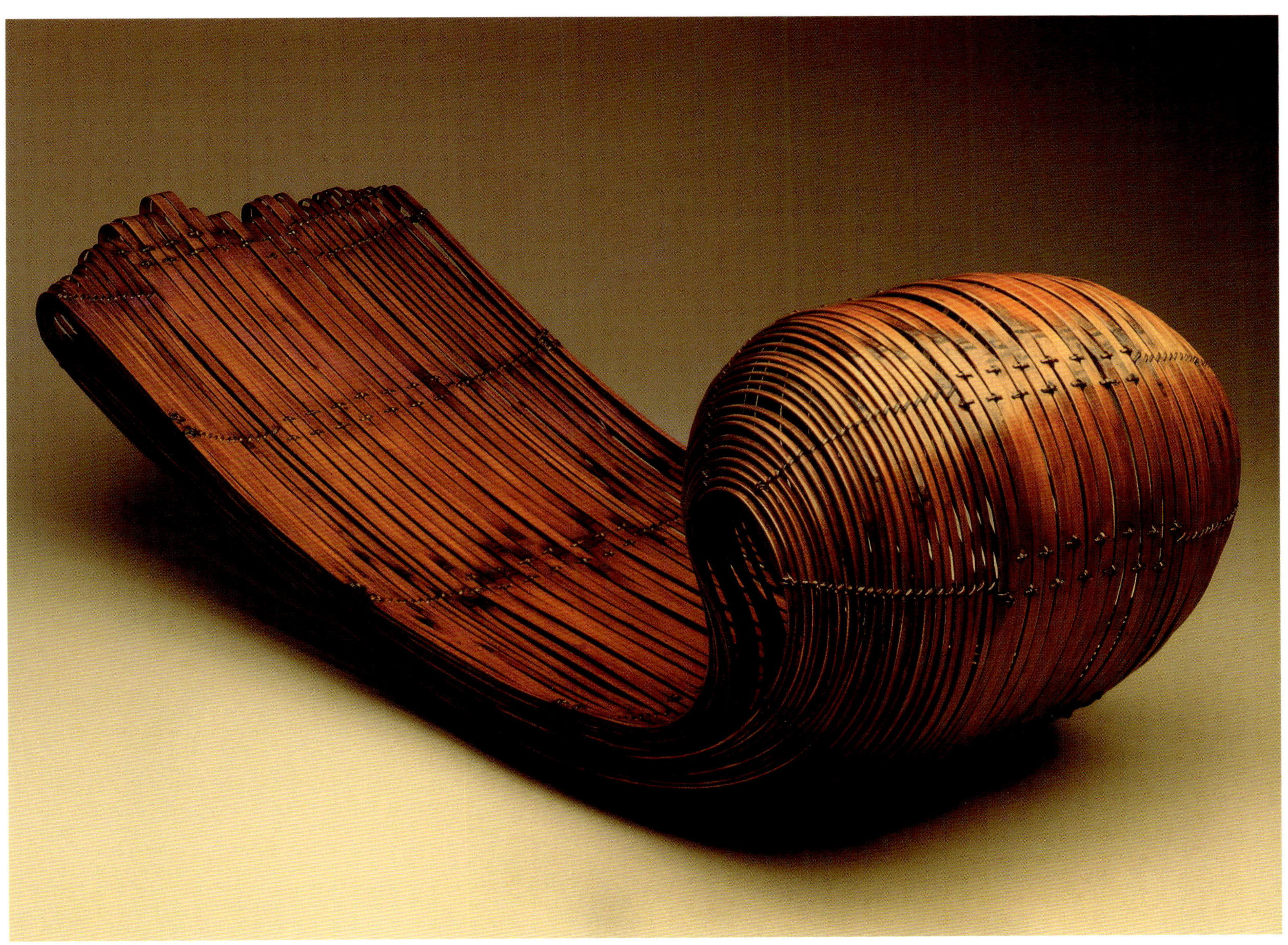

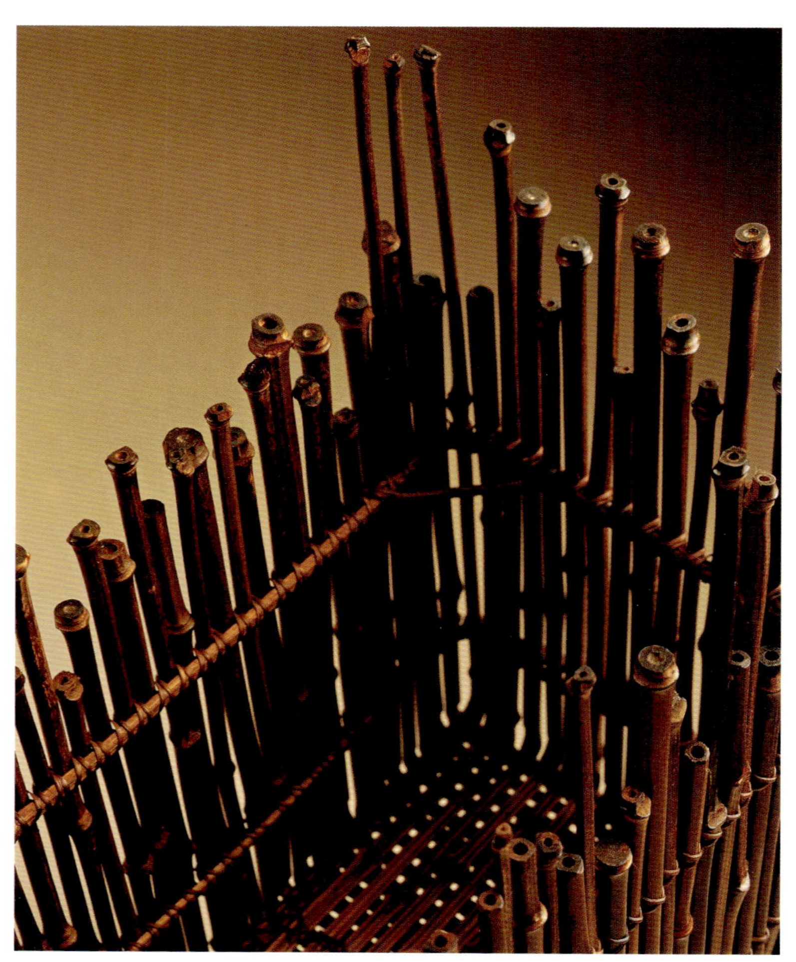

Fish Trap

1988

13" x 6 1/2" x 12" (33 x 17 x 30 cm)

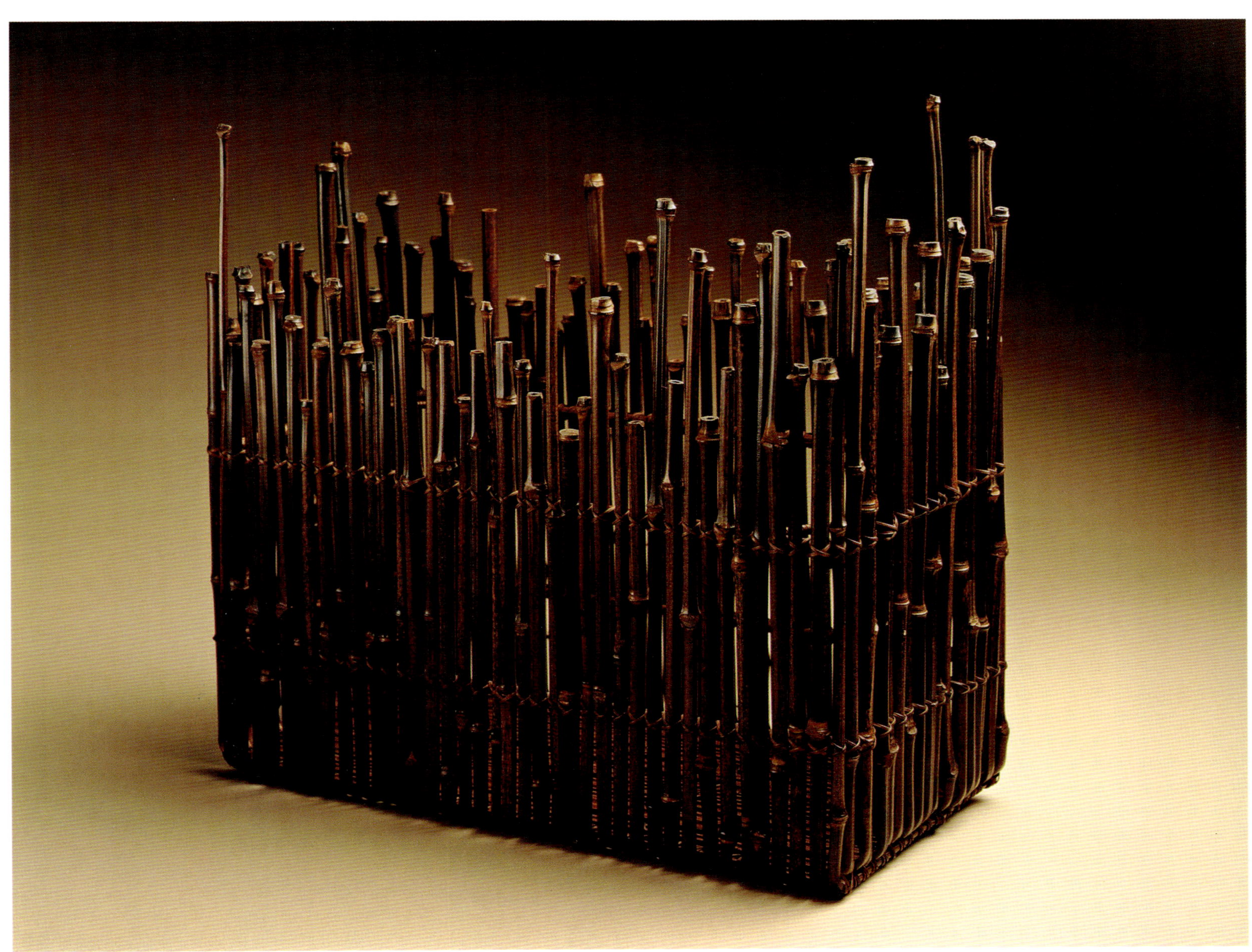

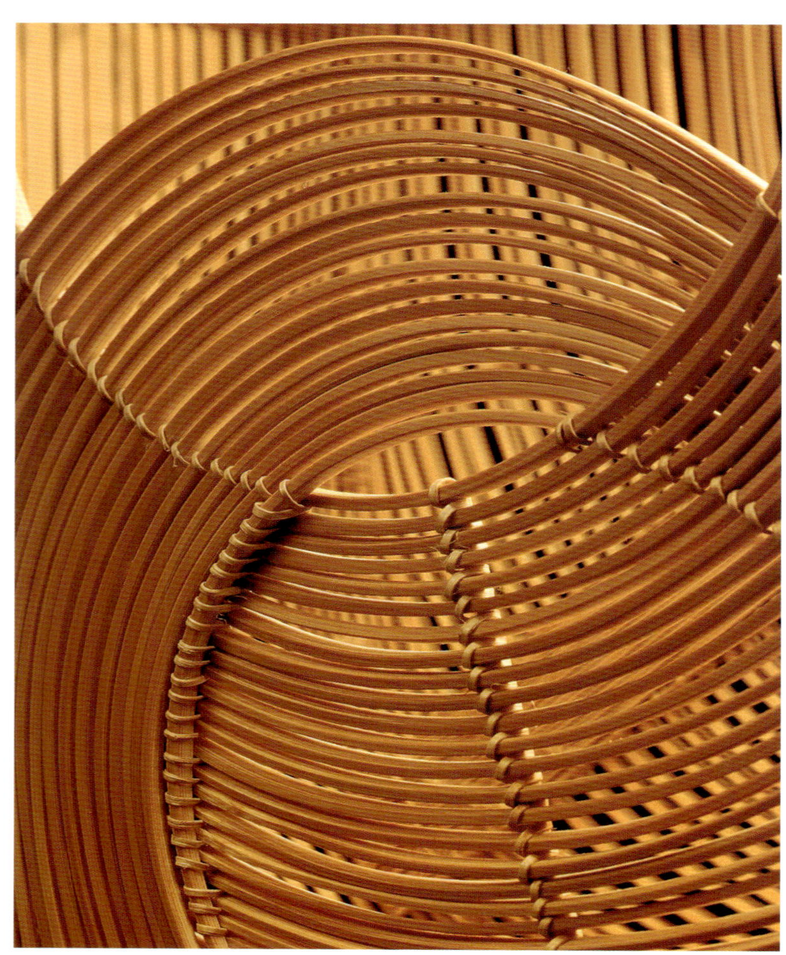

Wave

1988
16 1/2" x 25" x 10" (42 x 64 x 25 cm)

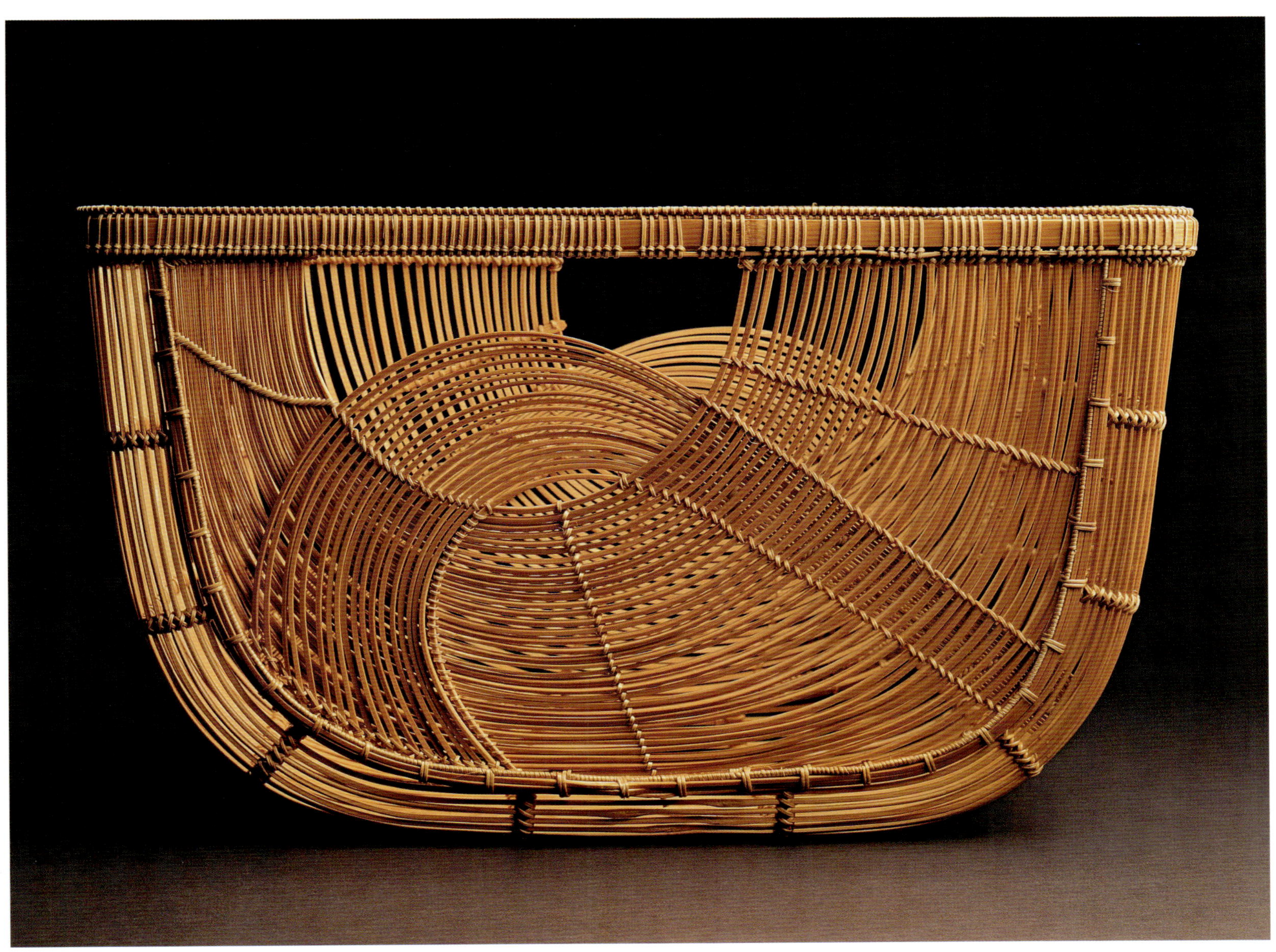

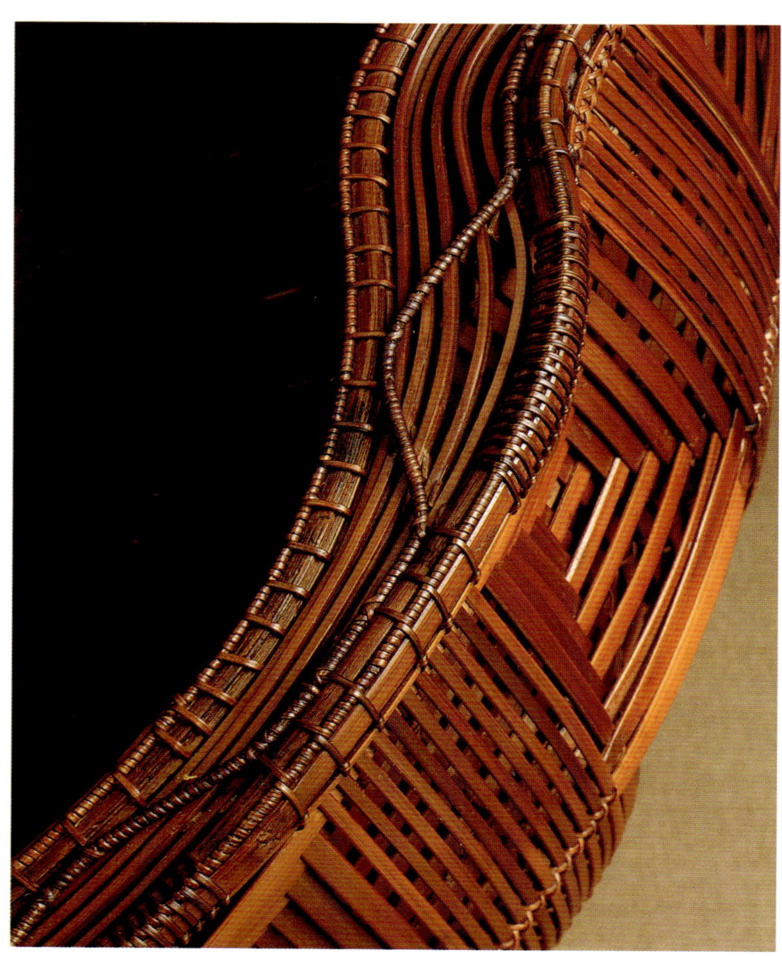

Sound Of The Ocean

1988
20"d x 7" (51d x 18 cm)

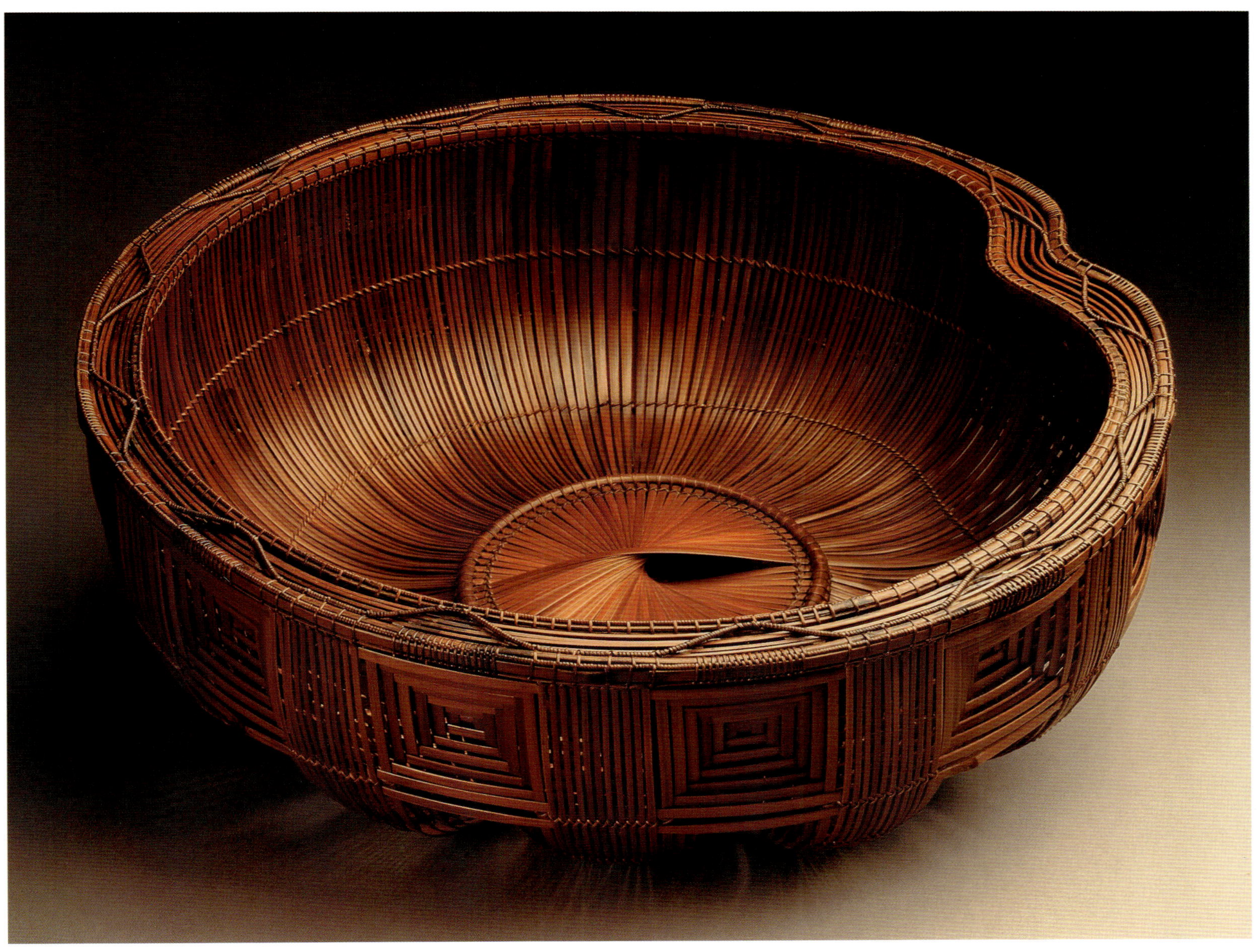

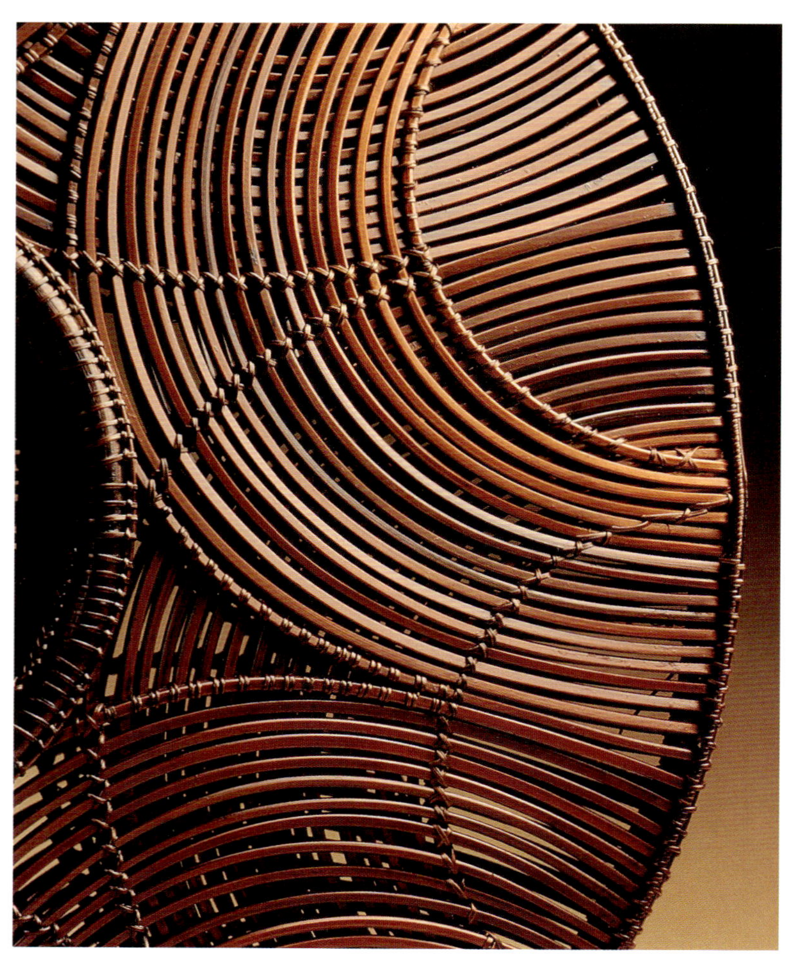

Ocean Waves Around Japan

1991
17 1/2" x 7" (44 x 18 cm)

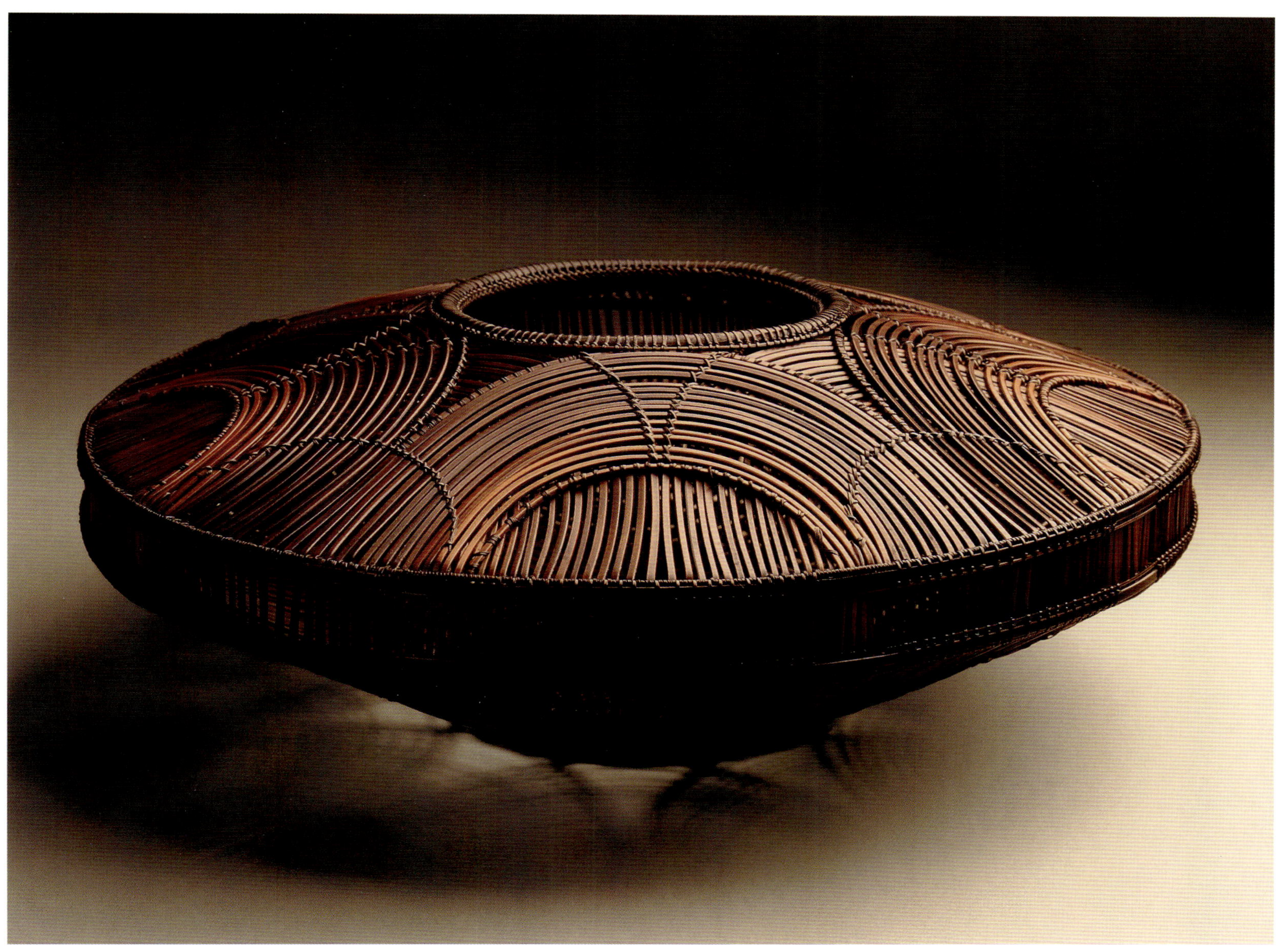

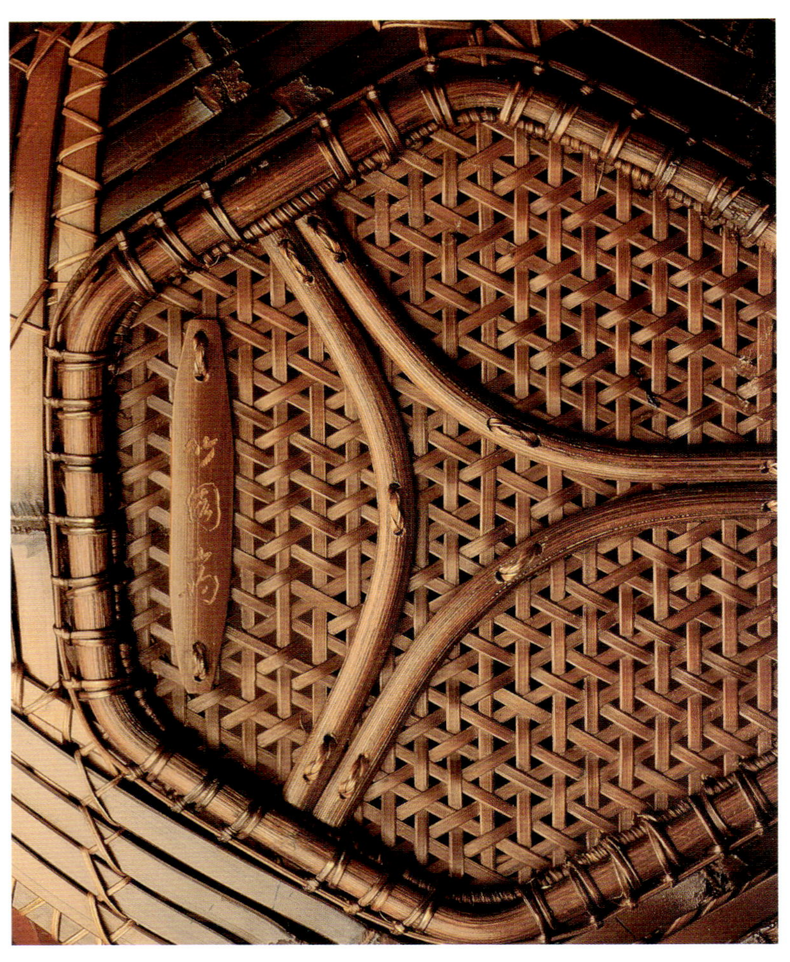

Cross-over Pattern Flower Basket

1993
10"d x 9" (25 x 23 cm)

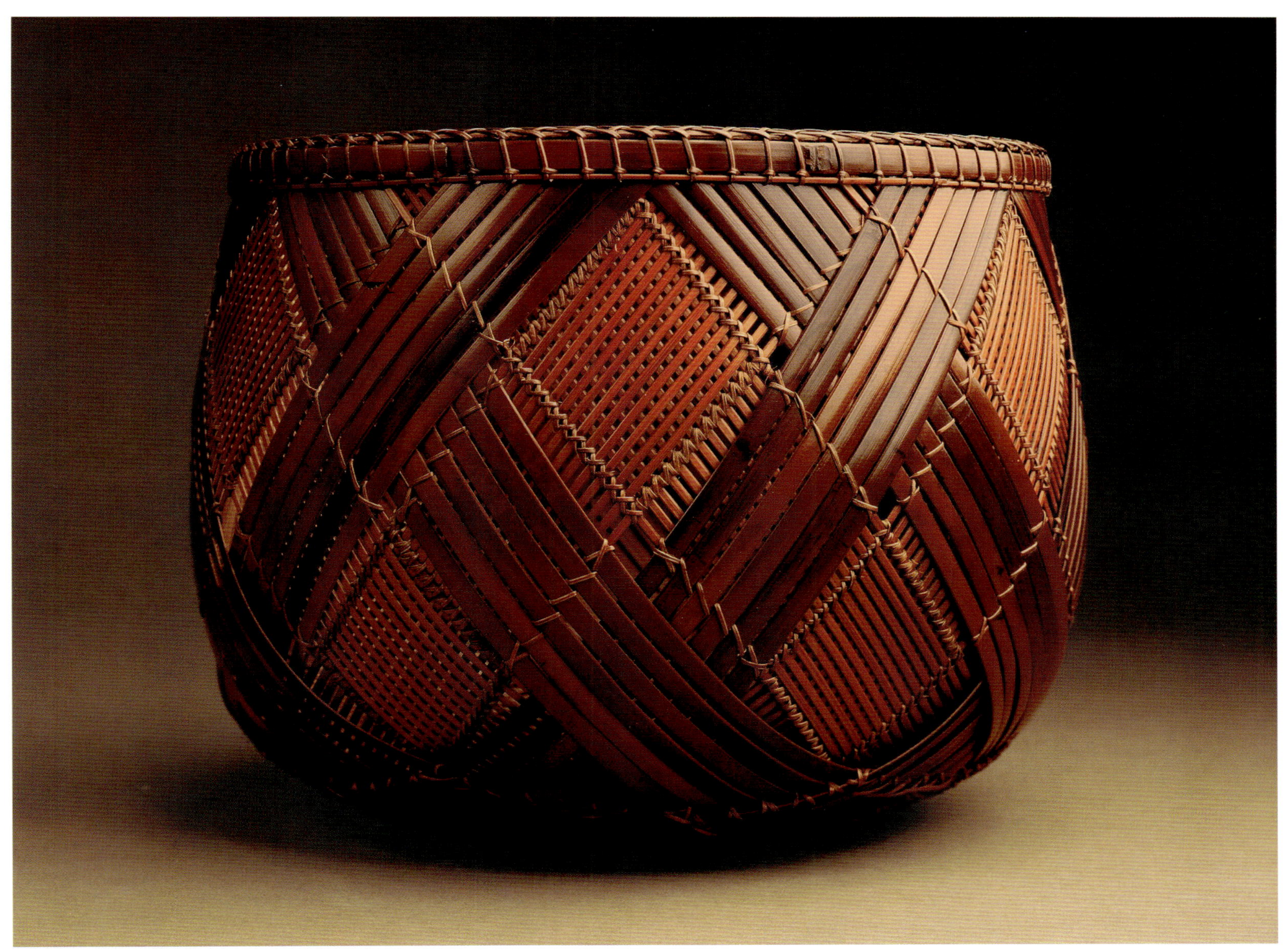

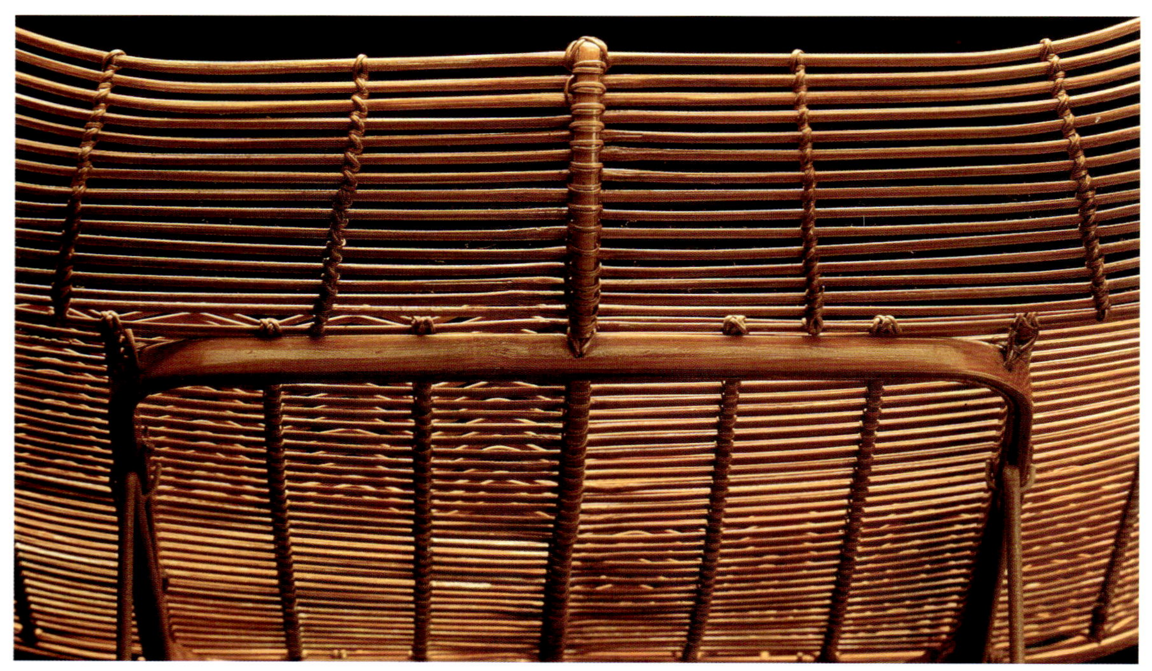

Small Waves

1997
20" x 14" x 4" (51 x 35 x 37 cm)

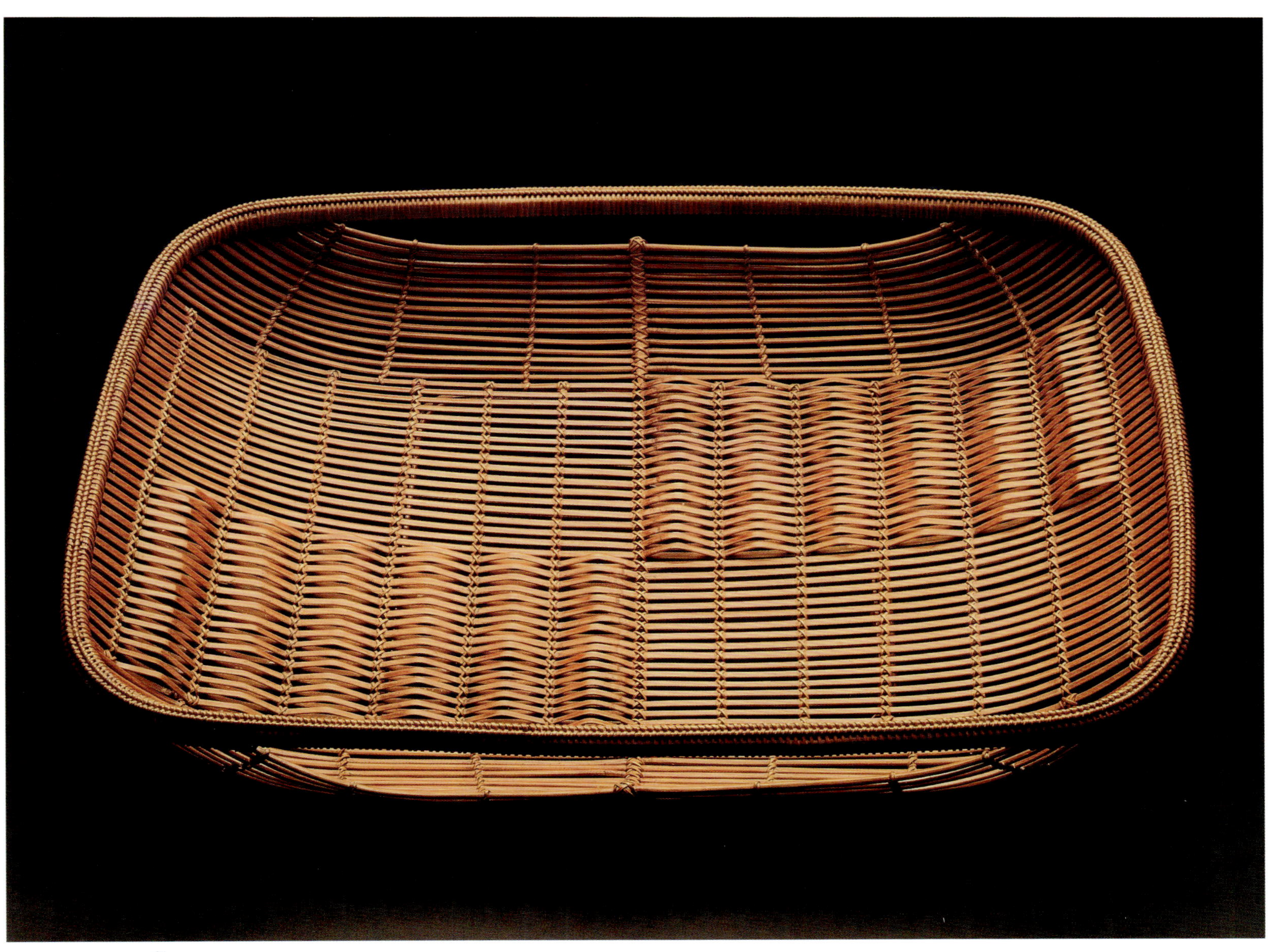

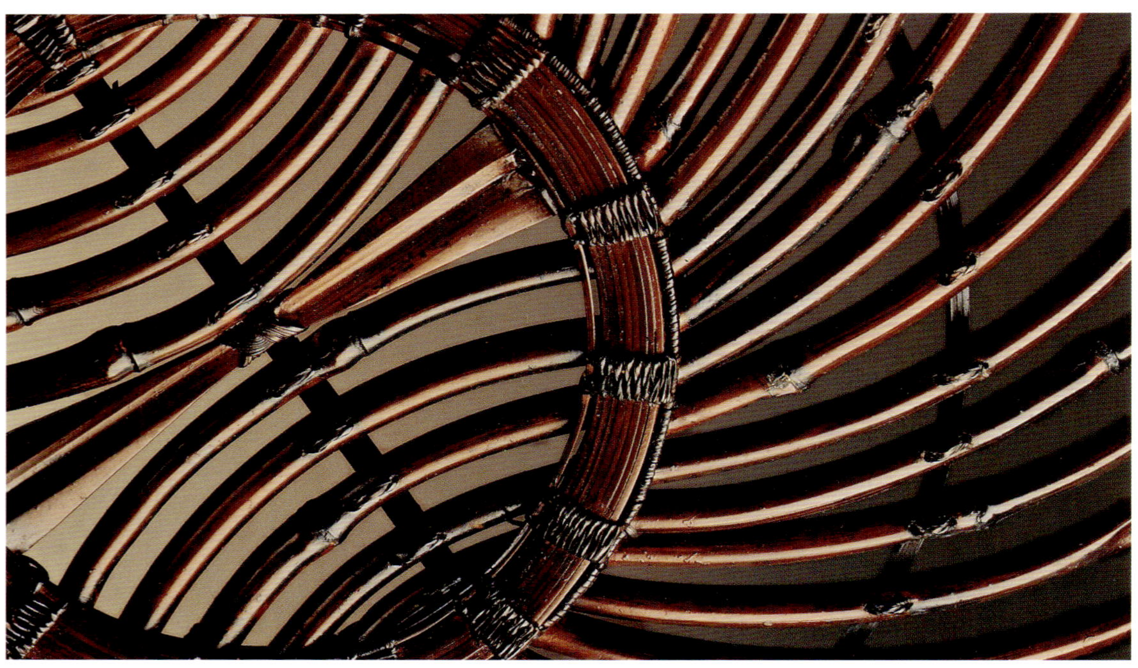

Sound of Water

2000
18"d x 5" (45d x 12 cm)

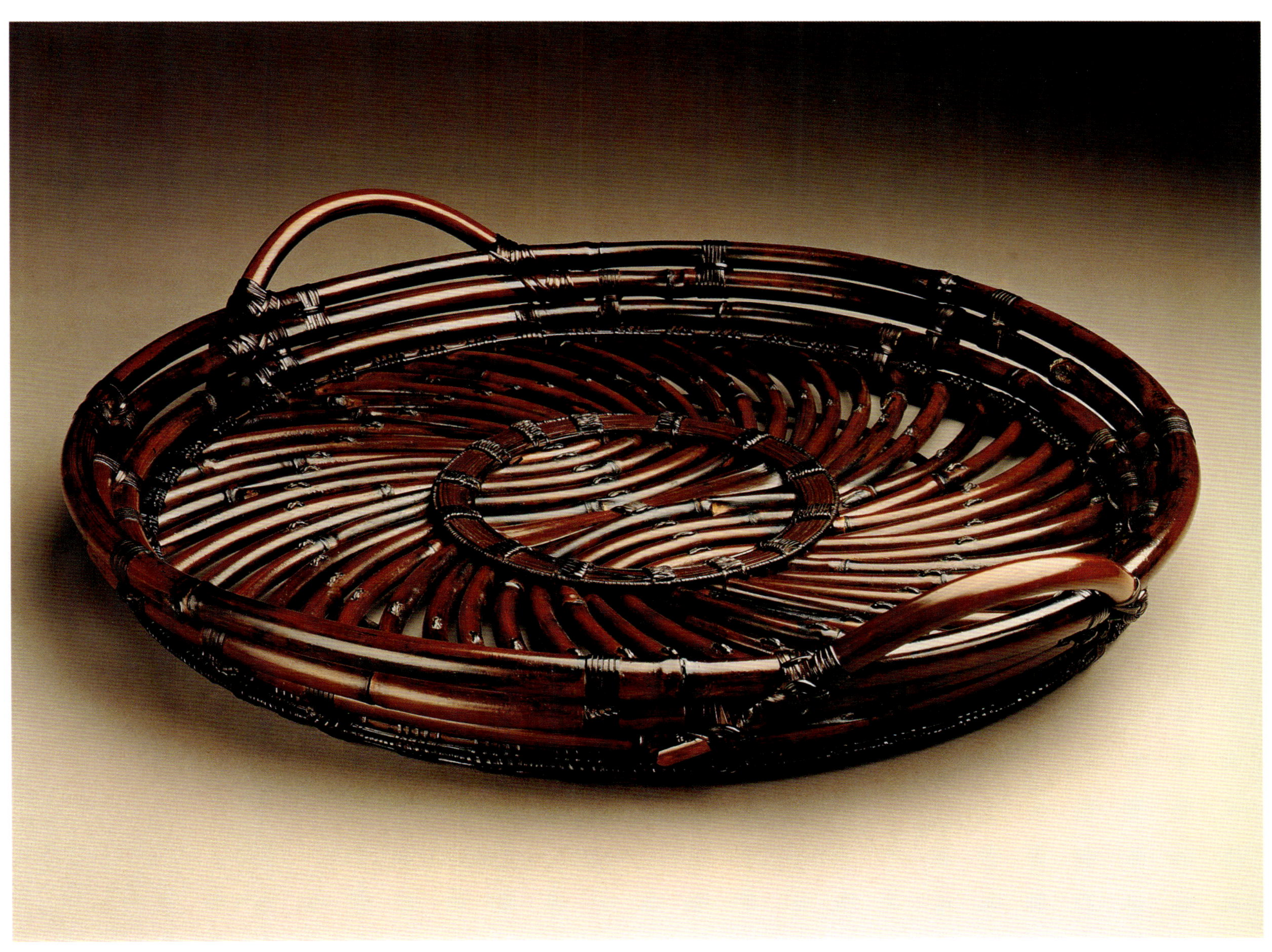

Appendix: Questions asked of Higashi Takesonosai

by Lloyd Cotsen

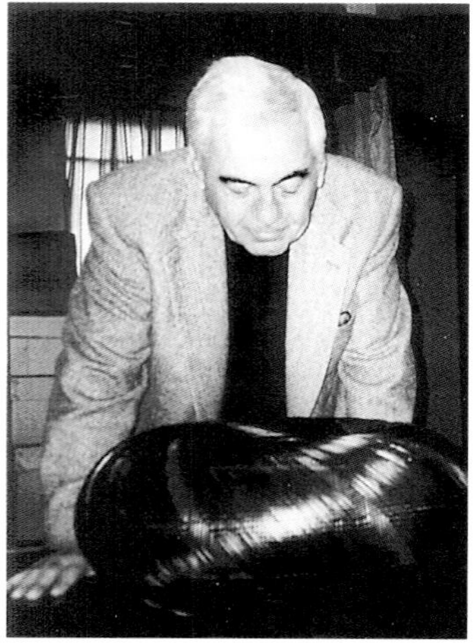

Lloyd Cotsen

What do you think about the future of bamboo arts in Japan?

Thinking about bamboo art in the future is a headache. I have heard that a Japanese collector is getting a little interested to buying bamboo work. Hearing about Mr. Cotsen's great collection and activities such as the Cotsen Bamboo Prize is a positive influence on young artists. Also, Mr. Coffland lately has been doing a lot to promote bamboo art in America and Japan. I am feeling a little more optimistic about bamboo artwork in the future.

Why have you never had an apprentice?

In order to create great artistic works for the future, I decided that having an apprentice would be a distraction. It is a great responsibility day to day for many years. However, when young artists asked me to help them, I try to show them what point is important, and I encouraged them to create original works. For instance, I gave advice to Noguchi Ramposai every weekend for a year or so in the 1970's.

Do you think you are a better artist than teacher?

Yes, both of my teachers were artisans and had no ideas about making original bamboo artwork. My ideas about bamboo is to use all of my ability to create art works and to be in a different world from my teachers.

Who do you most admire among younger bamboo artists?

There are two artists: the first is Tanioka Shigeo, who lives in the Kansai area. He studied under Tanabe Chikuunsai II from whom he learned excellent technique. The other artist is Katsushiro Soho, who lives in the Kanto region. He is someone who actively seeks other artistic experiences, which is so important for expanding one's artistic vision. I hope there will be other bamboo artists who will blossom.

Does the government have any responsibility to preserve bamboo art as an art form? Training of artists?

Yes, many of my works were exhibited at Nitten and Dento Kogei and have been collected by Kyoto Shiryokan museum. The Ministry of Culture has also purchased my bamboo baskets for museums. None of the art universities in Kyoto have any bamboo art classes, which is unfortunate. The government should do more.

In the future, where would you like your baskets to be — in museums or in private collections?

I am very happy people collect my work for their private collections. However, I also hope some pieces will go into museum collections for the public to enjoy.

Have you saved any drawings of your work?

No, I don't save drawings and models. I think if a work is completed, the drawing or model is not necessary any more.

How do you go from the idea of a basket to the finished artwork?

The character of the individual culms of bamboo gives me inspiration and direction. According to this, I start planning what I want to make. For the completed work to be successful, I first work on color aesthetics; second, technical aesthetics; third, form aesthetics; fourth, artistic beauty; and fifth, personality aesthetics. In this process, I try to use all of my human ability.

Which gives you the most pleasure as an artist — winning a major prize such as a Toksen, a museum acquiring your work, or a private collector acquiring your work?

To win a major prize such as Toksen is considered a gateway to success for an artist in the Japanese society. It is kind of like receiving a degree. Even if you make a great work that wins a Toksen, the value of the work comes by someone loving and appreciating it. And I wish more people will collect and love my work.

Should bamboo art strictly be just bamboo and rattan? Or should there be a return to the idea of other materials, like Shono Shounsai used in his Nitten work?

When Shono created a morikago for Nitten, he needed to use cherry tree bark at the corner of the edge in order complete his work. That part was impossible to be finish using either bamboo or rattan. In order to complete an artwork, it might be necessary for me to use another material with characteristics that bamboo or rattan do not have. Otherwise, I think it's not necessary to use other materials. It is the choice of the individual artist.

Does you think any other culture could threaten Japan's preeminence (in bamboo art)?

I do not think so. Japan has a unique culture without a parallel, and there is a mysterious attachment to bamboo.

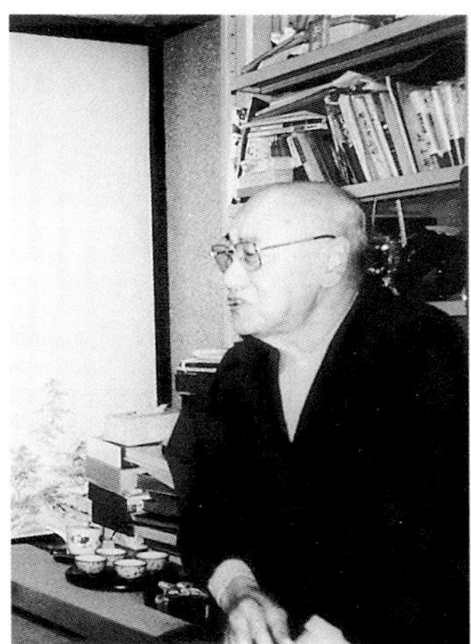

Higashi Takesonosai

Bibliography

Bess, Nancy Moore *Bamboo in Japan.* Tokyo: Kodansha International, 2001.

Coffland, Robert T. *Japanese Contemporary Bamboo Arts.* Chicago and Santa Fe: Art Media Resources and Tai Gallery, 1999.

Coffland, Robert T. "Japanese Bamboo Arts." *Arts of Asia*, Volume 29, Number 2, 1999.

Coffland, Robert T. "Energy and Strength in Balance: The Bamboo Basket Art of Fujinuma Noboru." *Orientations*, Volume 30, Number 2, February 1999.

Cort, Louise Allison, and Nakamura Kenji. *A Basketmaker in Rural Japan.* Washington D.C. and New York: Smithsonian Institution and Weatherhill, 1994.

Cotsen, Lloyd, Janet Koplos, Patricia J. Graham, Hiroko Johnson, and Moroyama Masanori. Edited by Joseph N. Newland. *Masterworks of Form and Texture: Japanese Bamboo Baskets.* Los Angeles: Cotsen Occasional Press, 1999.

Farrelly, David. *The Book of Bamboo.* San Francisco: Sierra Club Books, 1984.

Kahlenberg, Mary Hunt, and Mark Schwartz. *A Book About Grass: Its Beauty and Uses.* New York: E.P. Dutton, 1983.

Kaneko Kenji and Moroyama Masanori. *Take no kogei: kindai ni okeru tenkai* (Modern bamboo craft: Developments in the modern era). Tokyo: Tokyo National Museum of Modern Art, 1985.

McCallum, Toshiko M. *Containing Beauty: Japanese Bamboo Flower Baskets.* Los Angeles: UCLA Museum of Cultural History, 1988.

Lloyd Cotsen In addition to being a passionate collector of Japanese bamboo baskets, Lloyd Cotsen continues to seriously collect illustrated children's books and textiles. To this effect, he has supported the founding of the Cotsen Children's Library at Princeton University, the Cotsen Wing at the Museum of International Folk Art in Santa Fe, and the Cotsen Institute of Archaeology at UCLA, and a foundation for the art of teaching. A graduate of Princeton University, Mr. Cotsen served in the Navy as a Lt. JG and was then a Fellow of the American School of Classical Studies in Athens, Greece. He received an MBA from Harvard Business School and holds honorary doctor degrees from Pepperdine University and the University of Cincinnati. Up to 1994, he was president and chief executive officer of Neutrogena Corporation until it was sold. He and his wife live in Los Angeles near his three children and six grandchildren.

Robert T. Coffland first visited Japan in 1982. He has curated with his wife, Mary Hunt Kahlenberg, two exhibitions in Japan on American Indian and African art. Their Tai Gallery is involved in developing and curating public and private art collections in the United States, Europe, and Asia. Coffland is a writer, lecturer, and researcher on Japanese bamboo arts, and currently serves on the New Mexico Arts Commission. He is the author of *Japanese Contemporary Bamboo Arts*. He lives in Santa Fe, New Mexico.

Pat Pollard studied photography at Columbia College, Chicago. As a commercial photographer on the East Coast, she won numerous awards for her work. Pollard was the photographer for *The Extraordinary in the Ordinary: Textiles and Objects from the Collections of Lloyd Cotsen and the Neutrogena Corporation, Masterworks of Form and Texture: Japanese Bamboo Baskets and Japanese Contemporary Bamboo Arts*. She is also an artist who works in mixed media. Pollard lives in Rancho de Taos, New Mexico.

Art Streiber is a freelance photographer who specializes in travel, reportage, and entertainment portraiture. Streiber is a regular contributor to *Vanity Fair, In Style, Time, W, Town & Country*, and *Departures*. His portraits appear in *Japanese Contemporary Bamboo Arts*. He lives in Los Angeles.

All the pieces in the book are in the Lloyd Cotsen Japanese Bamboo Basket collection, except for pages 20, 22, 24, 26, 28, 32, 42, 76, 96, 98 which are in Higashi's personal collection.

Japanese names are given in traditional order, surname first.
For example, "Higashi" is the family name in Higashi Takesonosai.

The character for Higashi can also be read as Azuma.
Higashi does not refer to himself as Azuma.

Editor: Rochelle Reed
Translation: Yoneyama Yoshiko and Okada Koichiro
Design, production and printing: CA Design, Hong Kong

Published by COTSEN OCCASIONAL PRESS
Los Angeles, California

Distributed by Art Media Resources, Ltd.
1507 South Michigan Avenue, Chicago, IL 60605
info@artmediaresources.com
www.artmediaresources.com

ISBN: 1-58886-025-6 Hardcover
ISBN: 1-58886-026-4 Softcover

Front Cover: "Sound Of The Ocean" 1988 20"d x 7" (51d x 18 cm)
Back Cover: "Iris Pattern Flower Basket" 1954 17" x 16" x 10" (43 x 41 x 26 cm)